John R. Sweney

Temple Trio

John R. Sweney

Temple Trio

ISBN/EAN: 9783337779023

Printed in Europe, USA, Canada, Australia, Japan

Cover: Foto ©Thomas Meinert / pixelio.de

More available books at **www.hansebooks.com**

Looking unto Jesus.—CONCLUDED.

Looking un-to Je-sus, O- ver all the armor Faith the battle shield.

5 I will Trust in Thee.

In answer to question of leader at Ocean Grove "Who will trust?" many rose, saying, "I will."

W. H. G.   W. H. GEISTWEIT.

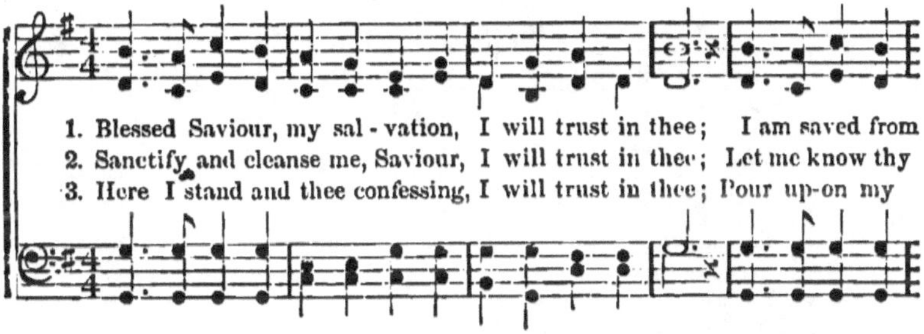

1. Blessed Saviour, my sal-vation, I will trust in thee; I am saved from
2. Sanctify and cleanse me, Saviour, I will trust in thee; Let me know thy
3. Here I stand and thee confessing, I will trust in thee; Pour up-on my

CHORUS.

condemn-a-tion, I will trust in thee. Yes, I will, yes, I will,
lov-ing fa-vor, I will trust in thee.
heart thy blessing, I will trust in thee.

I will trust in thee; Thou, my Strength and Song forever, I will trust in thee.

Copyright, 1886, by JOHN J. HOOD.

They are Coming.—CONCLUDED.

They are coming, they are coming, Hallelujah! they are coming home to rest.

---

13. Ever Singing.

Mrs. E. C. Ellsworth. "With songs and everlasting joy"—Isa. xxxv. 10.   S. J. Robson.

1. On my way to Zi - on Songs my lips em - ploy; Ev - er fresh the
2. Songs of joy be - fore me Shall my soul in - cite, For I'm pressing
3. God my hand is hold - ing, And a song he gives, With the sweet as-
4. When with foes I'm fighting For the vic - to - ry, Songs of great de-

CHORUS.

good - ness, Ev - er new the joy.   I am ev - er sing - ing,
on - ward To the gold - en light.
sur - ance, My Redeem - er lives.
liv - 'rance Set my spir - it free.

Singing all the way; Singing thro' the darkness, Singing thro' the day.

Copyright, 1881, by John J. Hood.   From "The Wells of Salvation," by per.

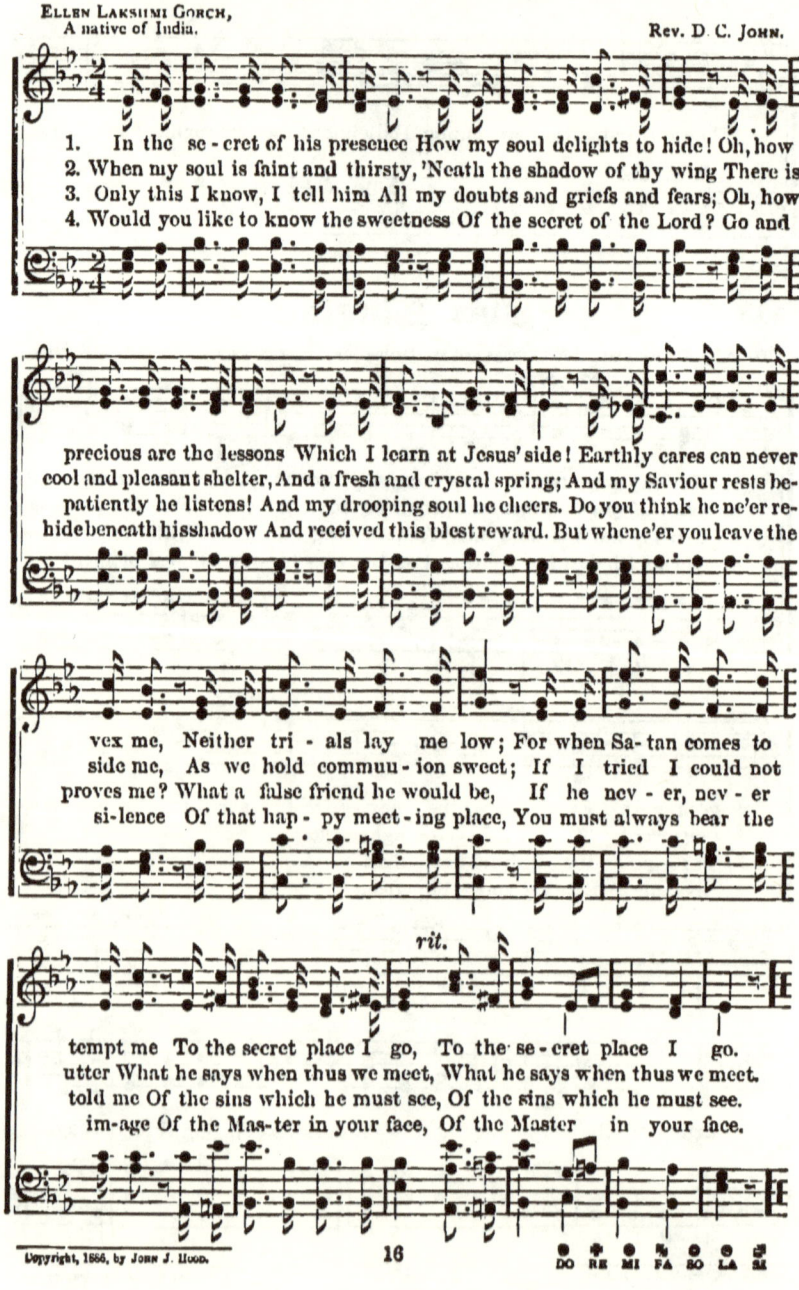

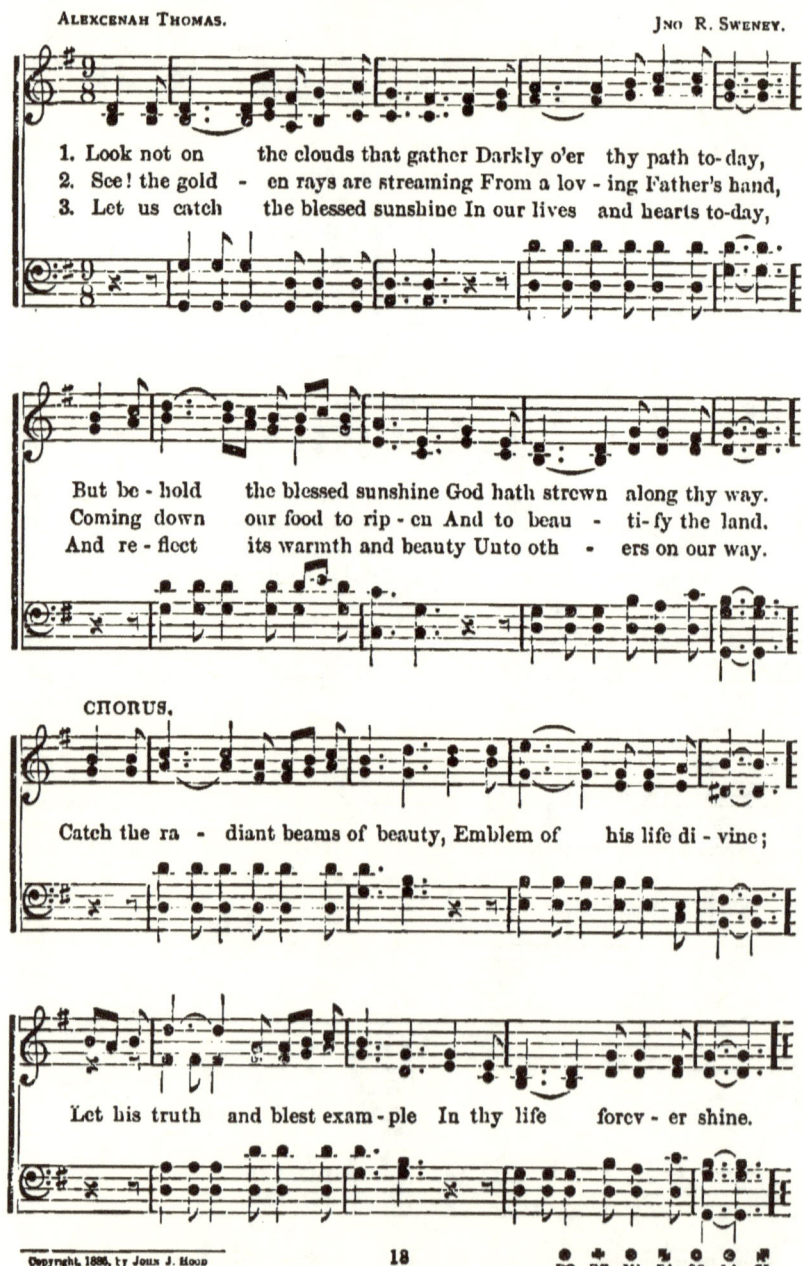

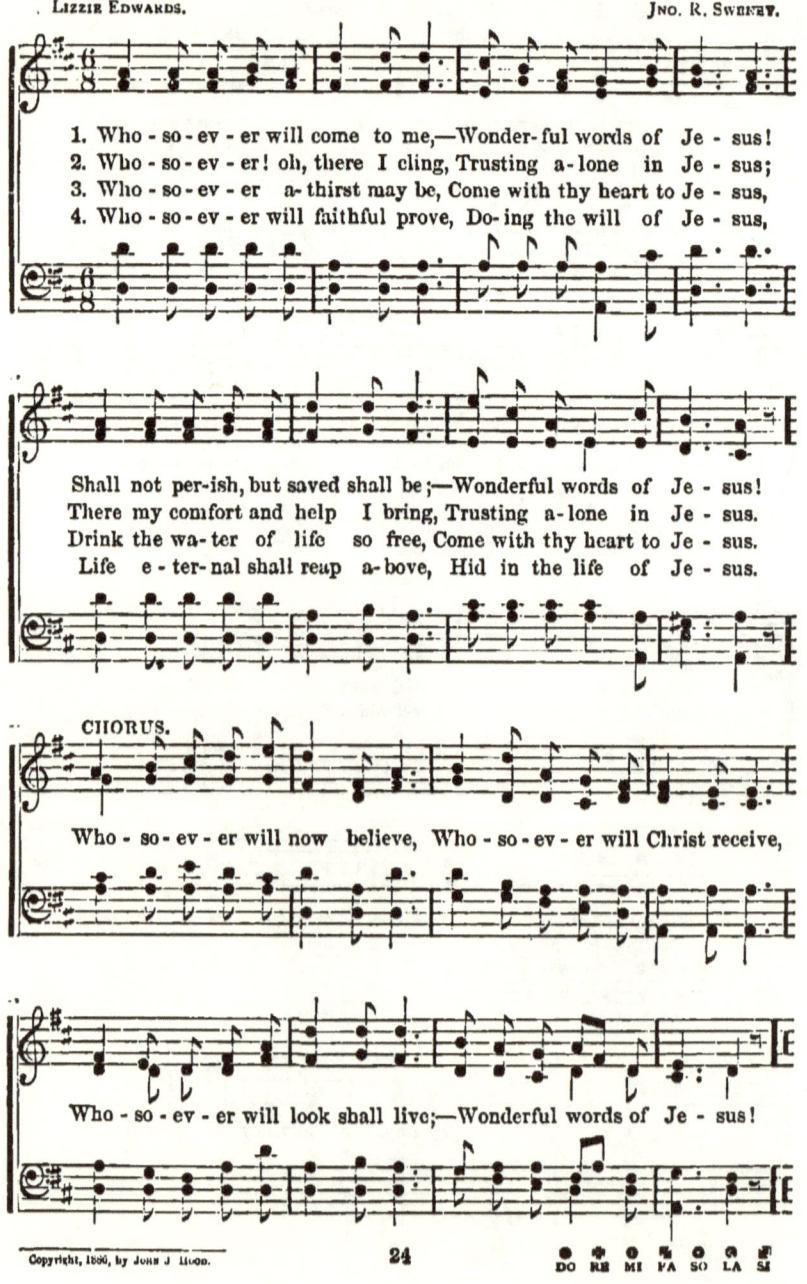

Making Melody.—CONCLUDED.

Repeat pp.

I will sing, I will sing, Making melo-dy un-to the Lord.

25. Care for the Desolate.

FRANK GOULD. J. R. S.

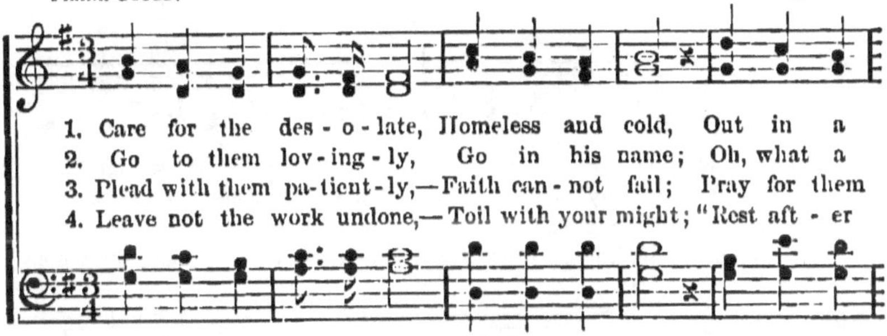

1. Care for the des-o-late, Homeless and cold, Out in a
2. Go to them lov-ing-ly, Go in his name; Oh, what a
3. Plead with them pa-tient-ly,—Faith can-not fail; Pray for them
4. Leave not the work undone,—Toil with your might; "Rest aft-er

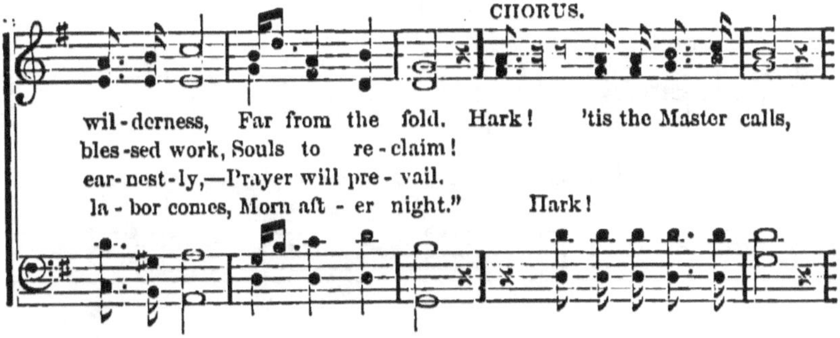

CHORUS.

wil-derness, Far from the fold. Hark! 'tis the Master calls,
bles-sed work, Souls to re-claim!
ear-nest-ly,—Prayer will pre-vail.
la-bor comes, Morn aft-er night." Hark!

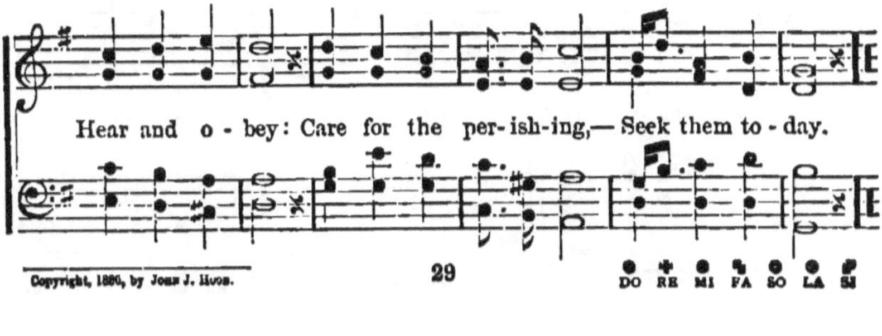

Hear and o-bey: Care for the per-ish-ing,—Seek them to-day.

Copyright, 1886, by JOHN J. HOOD.

DO RE MI FA SO LA SI

28. Nearer, my God, to Thee.

Tune above.

1 NEARER, my God, to thee!
  Nearer to thee,
 E'en though it be a cross
  That raiseth me;
 Still all my song shall be,
 Nearer, my God, to thee,
  Nearer to thee!

2 Though like the wanderer,
  The sun gone down,
 Darkness be over me,
  My rest a stone,
 Yet in my dreams I'd be
 Nearer, my God, to thee,
  Nearer to thee!

3 There let the way appear,
  Steps unto heaven;
 All that thou sendest me,
  In mercy given;

 Angels to beckon me
 Nearer, my God, to thee,
  Nearer to thee!

4 Then with my waking thoughts
  Bright with thy praise,
 Out of my stony griefs
  Bethel I'll raise,
 So by my woes to be
 Nearer, my God, to thee,
  Nearer to thee!

5 Or if on joyful wing
  Cleaving the sky,
 Sun, moon, and stars forgot,
  Upward I fly,
 Still all my song shall be
 Nearer, my God, to thee,
  Nearer to thee!

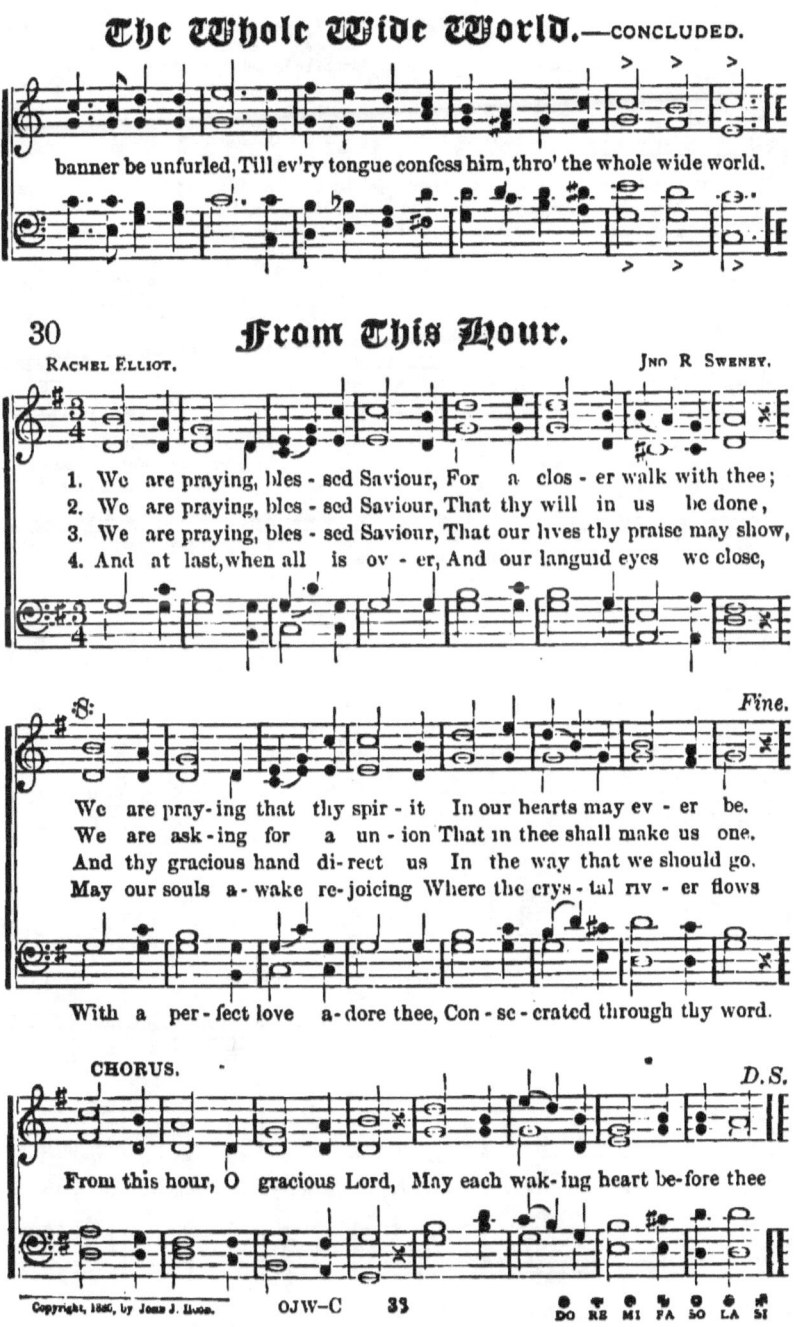

34. Drinking at the Fountain.

MATILDA C. DAY.   WM. J. KIRKPATRICK.

1. We are drinking at the fount-ain Of redeeming, precious love;
2. We are drinking at the fount-ain That for all so free-ly flows,
3. At the blessed, living fount-ain, Ev-er flowing, bright and clear,
4. When we reach our Father's Kingdom, And our pilgrim life is o'er,

At the crystal fountain flow-ing From our Father's throne a-bove.
In the murmur of its wa-ters There's a balm for mor-tal woes.
There is joy for ev-'ry sor-row, And a smile for ev-'ry tear.
At the fountain pure and sparkling We will drink, and thirst no more.

CHORUS.

Yes, we're drinking at the fountain, The wonderful, wonderful fount-ain,

Drinking full salva-tion at the fount-ain Of life and redeeming love.

Copyright, 1880, by JOHN J. HOOD.

DO ME MI FA SO LA SI

The Universal Call. —CONCLUDED.

Come, The Bride says, Come, And drink of the water of life....
come, The Bride says, come, come, And drink of the water of life, And drink of the water of life.

44 Each Heart Thy Temple.

LAURA MILLER. JNO. R. SWENEY.

1. Thou chief among ten thousand, More love-ly far than all;
2. We come, as thou hast taught us, Thy mer-its, Lord, we plead,
3. We know that thou art with us, We feel thy power di-vine;
4. Our souls, and all with-in us, We con-se-crate to thee,

Re-veal thyself in glo-ry, While on thy name we call.
Be-cause thou liv-est ev-er, For us to in-ter-cede.
Thy Spir-it bear-eth wit-ness That we through grace are thine.
And pray that in our weak-ness Thine arm our strength may be.

D. S.—Now make each heart thy tem-ple, And there henceforth a-bide.

CHORUS. D. S.

Thou chief a-mong ten thousand, Our on-ly faith-ful Guide,

Copyright, 1886, by JOHN J. HOOD.

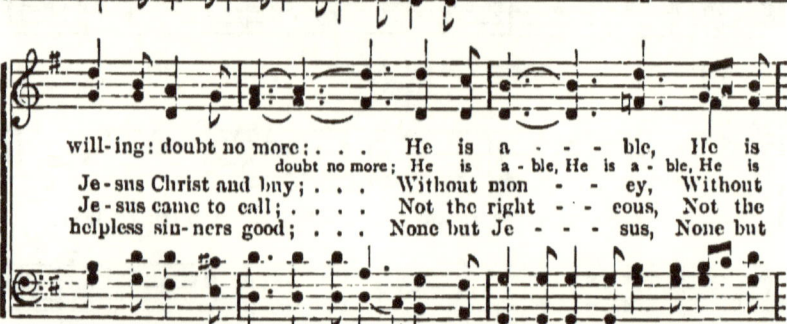

Come, ye Sinners.—CONCLUDED.

will - - ing, He is a - ble, He is willing: doubt no more.
will-ing, He is will-ing, He is will - ing: doubt no more.
mon - - ey, Without money, Come to Jesus Christ and buy.
right - - eous, Not the righteous,—Sinners Jesus came to call.
Je - - sus, None but Je-sus Can do helpless sin-ners good.

48 Remember Calvary.

CHAS. WESLEY. WM. J. KIRKPATRICK.

1. { Lamb of God, whose dy-ing love We now re-call to mind, }
   { Send the ans-wer from a-bove, And let us mer-cy find: }

Think on us who think on thee, And ev-'ry struggling soul re-lease;

O re-mem-ber Cal-va-ry, And bid us go in peace!

2 By thine agonizing pain,
  And bloody sweat, we pray,
  By thy dying love to man,
  Take all our sins away:
  Burst our bonds, and set us free;
  From all iniquity release;
  O remember Calvary,
  And bid us go in peace!

3 Let thy blood, by faith applied,
  The sinner's pardon seal;
  Speak us freely justified,
  And all our sickness heal:
  By thy passion on the tree,
  Let all our griefs and troubles [cease:
  O remember Calvary,
  And bid us go in peace!

49. When the Clouds were Dark.

Mrs. J. P. R. Perry.
Jno. R. Sweney.

1. When the clouds were dark above me, And I heard the billows roll,
2. When the fiercest storms were raging, And I found no earthly rest,
3. Let me hear thy voice, my Saviour, While I tread the vale of life;
4. Let my spir - it gladly fol-low Where thou lead-est day by day;

How the lov - ing voice of Je-sus Whispered com-fort to my soul!
Then my wea - ry head he pillowed On his kind and faithful breast.
Let me hear its tones so gentle 'Mid the con - flict and the strife.
When thou call - est, blessed Saviour, Let me nev - er answer, nay.

CHORUS.

Onward, then, I'll move in triumph, Till I reach the oth - er shore,

There to gath - er with the faithful, When the storms of life are o'er.

Copyright, 1886, by John J. Hood.

50. Have Mercy.

ADELAIDE A. PROCTER.   WM. J. KIRKPATRICK.

1. The way is long and dreary, The path is bleak and bare; Our feet are worn and weary, But we will not de-spair: More heavy was thy burden, More des-o-late thy way; O Lamb of God, who tak-est The sin of the world a-way: Have mercy, have mercy, Have mercy on us, we pray.

2. The snows lie thick around us, 'Tis dark and gloomy night; The tempest wails a-bove us, The stars have hid their light; But blacker was the darkness Round Calvary's cross that day; O Lamb of God, who tak-est The sin of the world a-way: Have mercy, have mercy, Have mercy on us, we pray.

3. Our hearts are faint with sorrow Heavy and hard to bear; We dread the bitter morrow, But we will not de-spair; Thou knowest all our anguish, And thou wilt bid it cease; O Lamb of God, we pray thee, Grant us thy joy and peace: Have mercy, have mercy, Grant us thy joy and peace.

Copyright, 1886, by JOHN J. HOOD.

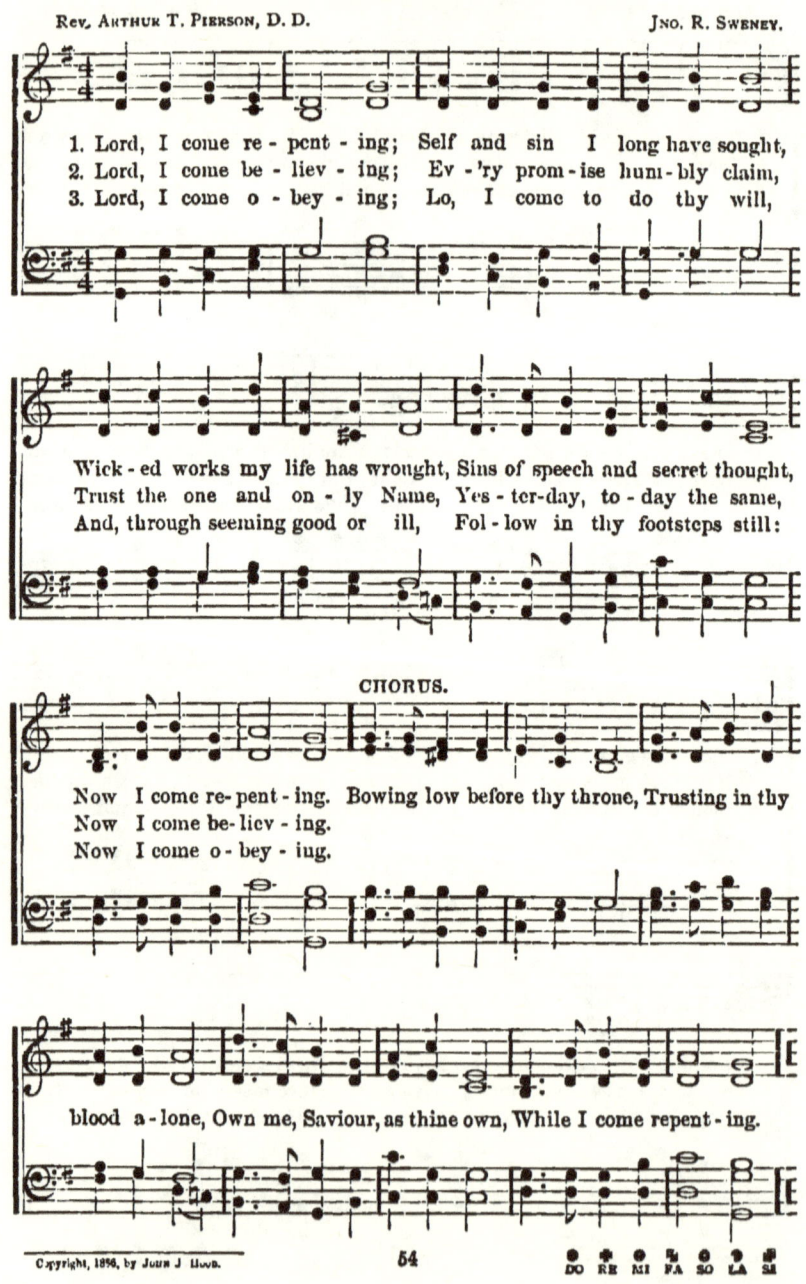

52. Redeemed, Praise the Lord.

ABBIE MILLS.   WM. J. KIRKPATRICK.

1. O happy day! what a Sav-iour is mine! I am redeemed, praise the Lord!
2. O clap your hands, all ye people of God, I am redeemed, praise the Lord!
3. Thanks be to God for the great vict'ry given, I am redeemed, praise the Lord!
4. Glory to God, I would shout ev-ermore, I am redeemed, praise the Lord!

Fine.

All to his pleasure I glad-ly re-sign, I am redeemed, praise the Lord!
Let ev'ry tongue speak his mercy abroad, I am redeemed, praise the Lord!
Now I am free; ev'ry chain has been riven,—I am redeemed, praise the Lord!
O for a voice that could reach ev'ry shore, I am redeemed, praise the Lord!

Key C.

Jesus has taken my burden away; Jesus has turned all my night into day;
His loving-kindness is better than gold; He doth bestow more than my cup can hold;
Out of the pit, and the mire, and the clay, Jesus has borne me in triumph away;
Help me, ye ransom'd, awake, ev'ry string, Let earth rejoice and the whole heavens ring,

Use first four lines as Chorus. D. C.

Jesus has come to my heart,—come to stay,—I am redeemed, praise the Lord!
Wondrous Salvation, that ne'er can be told,—I am redeemed, praise the Lord!
Safe on the rock I am standing to-day,—I am redeemed, praise the Lord!
While we the chorus u-ni-ted-ly sing, I am redeemed, praise the Lord!

Copyright, 1866, by JOHN J. HOOD.

54. The Strong One.

"Who is this from Edom, with dyed garments from Bozrah?"

Rev. Dwight Williams.   Dr. H. L. Gilmour.

1. Who is this from Edom With his garments dyed, In his strength and greatness, By the world denied? This is Christ the mighty, Strong alone to save, All his foes are conquered,—Victor o'er the grave. Give him praise forever; Give him throne and crown; Tell the world the story, Give the King renown!
2. Red is his appar-el; All the stains he wears Cover our transgressions— Sin of men he bears. From the wine-press trodden, Where he went alone, He hath brought salvation,—Grace to ev'ry one.
3. Hail the Lord of glo-ry! Hail the Saviour King; Let the people praise him; Let them tribute bring. Now the path is o-pen To the pearly gate; Go, ye ransomed sinners, For the price was great.

CHORUS.

Copyright, 1886, by John J. Hood.

The Cross and the Bible.—CONCLUDED.

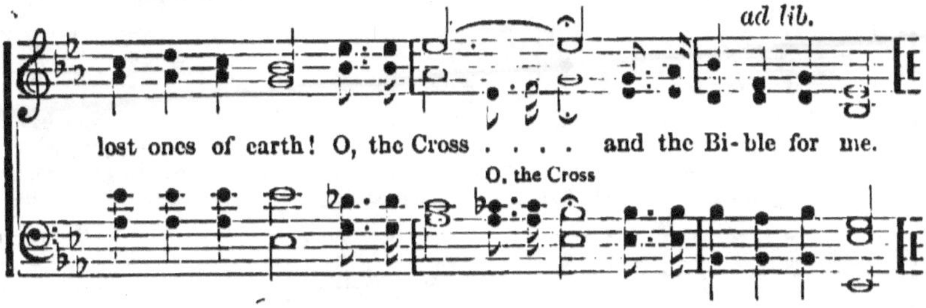

ad lib.
lost ones of earth! O, the Cross . . . . and the Bi-ble for me.
O, the Cross

56 Thou thinkest, Lord, of me.

E. D. MUND. "The Lord thinketh upon me."—Ps. xl. 17. E. S. LORENZ.

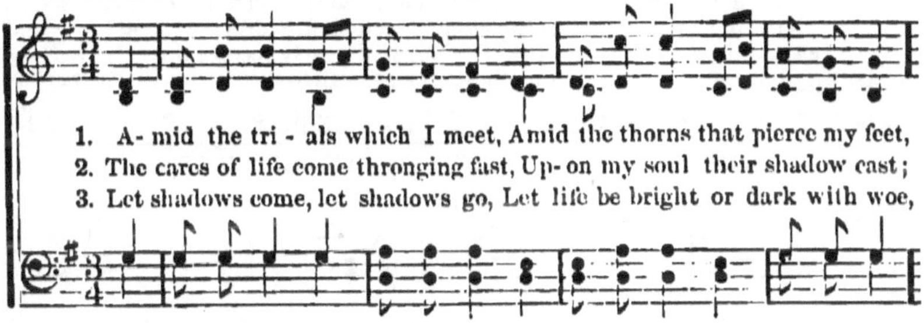

1. A-mid the tri - als which I meet, Amid the thorns that pierce my feet,
2. The cares of life come thronging fast, Up-on my soul their shadow cast;
3. Let shadows come, let shadows go, Let life be bright or dark with woe,

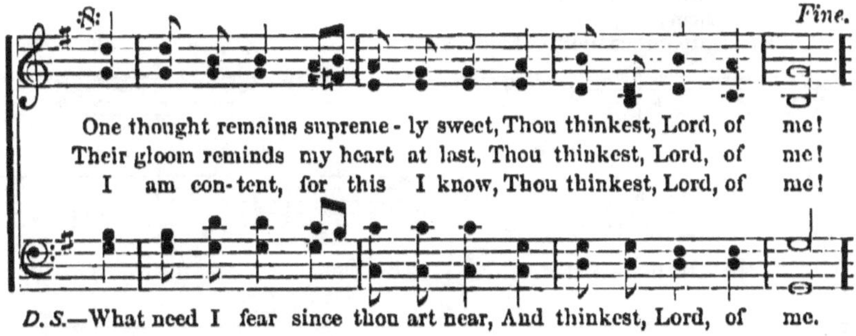

Fine.
One thought remains supreme - ly sweet, Thou thinkest, Lord, of me!
Their gloom reminds my heart at last, Thou thinkest, Lord, of me!
I am con-tent, for this I know, Thou thinkest, Lord, of me!
D. S.—What need I fear since thou art near, And thinkest, Lord, of me.

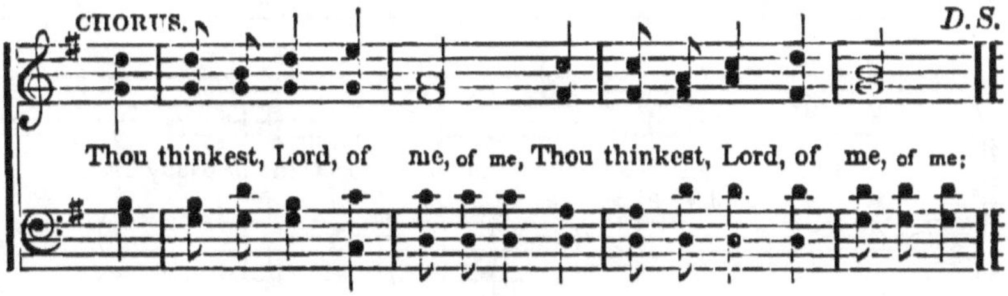

CHORUS.
D. S.
Thou thinkest, Lord, of me, of me, Thou thinkest, Lord, of me, of me;

By permission.

DO RE MI FA SO LA SI

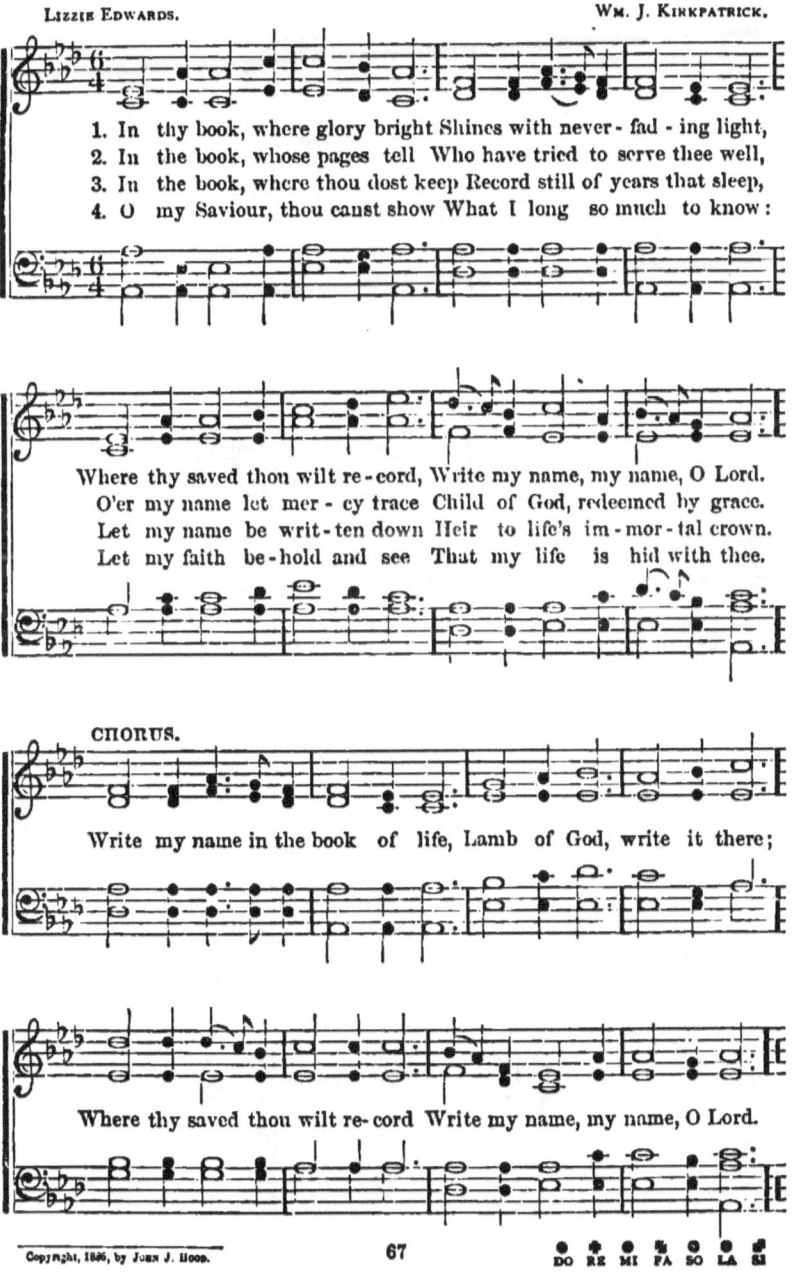

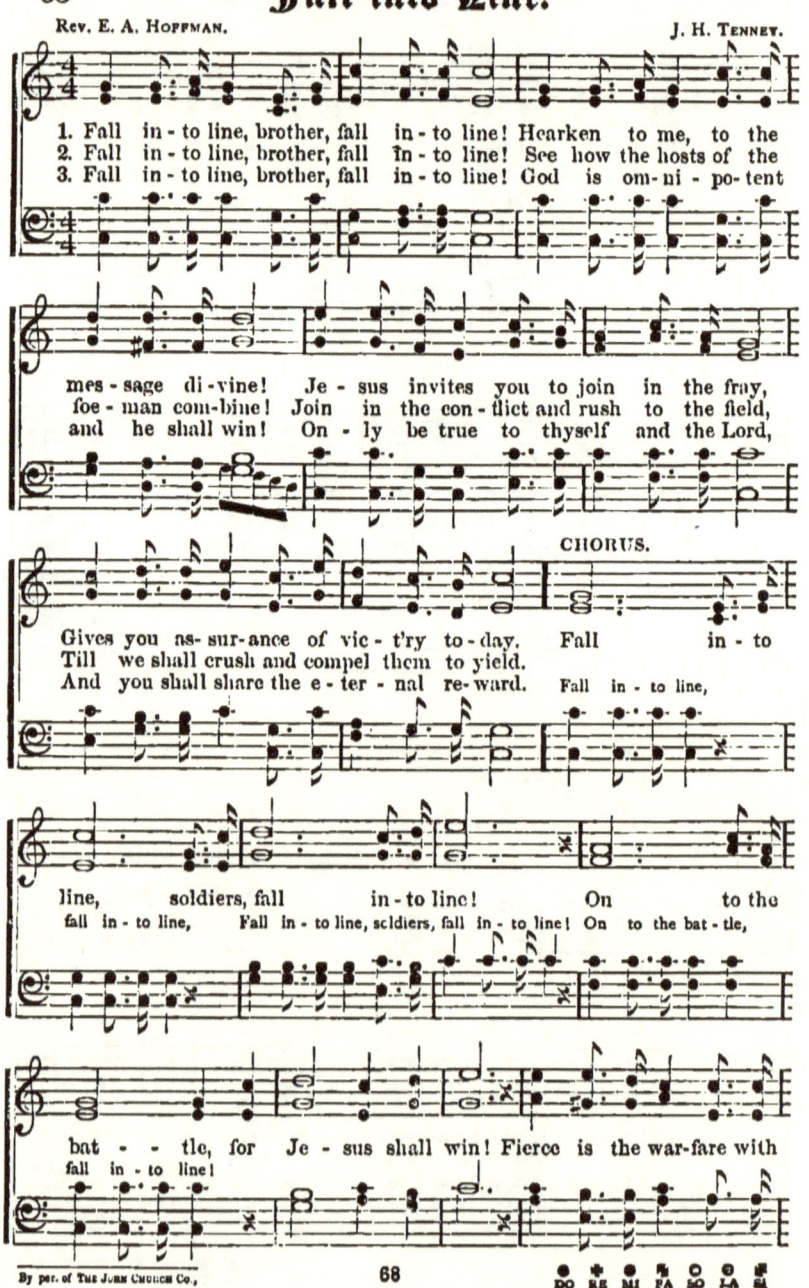

Fall into Line.—CONCLUDED.

Sa-tan to-day; Arm for the con-flict and march to the fray.

66. Eternity!—Where?

A young man was working alone in a large room in which was a big clock, the loud ticking of which seemed to frame itself into the words, "Eternity!—where?" Unable to endure any longer the reflections thus awakened, he arose and stopped the clock; but the question, "Eternity!—where?" still so haunted him, that he threw down his work, and hurrying home, determined that he would not allow anything to engage his thoughts till he could satisfactorily answer that searching question, "Eternity!—where?"

JNO. R. SWENEY.

1. "E-ter-nity!—where?" It floats in the air; Amid clam-or or si-lence it ev-er is there! The ques-tion so solemn—"E-ter-nity!—where?" The question so solemn—"E-ter-nity!—where?"
2. "E-ter-nity!—where?" Oh! Eternity!—where? With redeemed ones in glo-ry? or fiends in de-spair? With one or the oth-er—"E-ter-nity!—where?" With one or the oth-er—"E-ter-nity!—where?"
3. "E-ter-nity!—where?" Oh! how can you share The world's giddy pleasures, or heed-less-ly dare Do aught till you set-tle—"E-ter-nity!—where?" Do aught till you settle—"E-ter-nity!—where?"
4. "E-ter-nity!—where?" Oh! friend, have a care; Soon God will no long-er his judgment for-bear; This day may de-cide your "E-ter-nity!—where?" This day may decide your "E-ter-nity!—where?"
5. "E-ter-nity!—where?" Oh! Eter-nity!—where? Friend, sleep not, nor take in the world an-y share, Till you answer this question—"E-ter-nity!—where?" Till you answer this question—"Eternity!—where?"

Copyright, 1886, by JOHN J. HOOD.

70. Your Own.

L. G. M'VEAN.
LELIA WATERHOUSE.

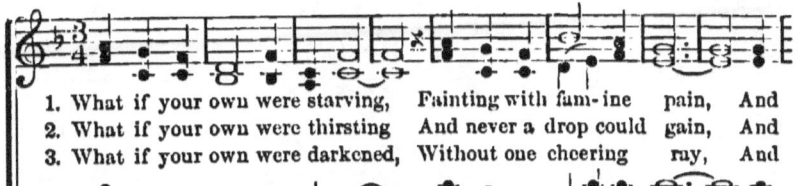

1. What if your own were starving, Fainting with fam-ine pain, And yet you knew where golden grew Rich fruit and ripened grain? Would you hear their wail As a thrice told tale, And turn to your feast again? feast again?
2. What if your own were thirsting And never a drop could gain, And you could tell where a sparkling well Poured forth melodious rain? Would you turn aside, While they gasped and died, And leave them to their pain? to their pain?
3. What if your own were darkened, Without one cheering ray, And you alone could show where shone The pure, sweet light of day? Would you leave them there In their dark despair, And sing on your sunlit way? sunlit way?

4 What if your own were wand'ring
  Far in a trackless maze,
And you could show them where to go
  Along your pleasant ways?
    Would your heart be light,
    Till the pathway right
Was plain before their gaze?

5 What if your own were prisoned
  Far in a hostile land,
And the only key to set them free
  Held in your safe command?
    Would you breathe free air,
    While they stifled there,
And wait, and hold your hand?

6 Yet, what else are you doing,
  O ye by Christ made free,
If you'll not tell what you know so well,
  To those across the sea,
    Who have never heard
    One tender word
Of the Lamb of Calvary?

7 "They're not our own," you answer,
  "They're neither kith nor kin."
They are God's own: his love alone
  Can save them from their sin;
    They are Christ's own:
    He left his throne
And died their souls to win.

Copyright, 1884, by JOHN J. HOOD.   From "Hymns of the Heart," by per.

The Handwriting, etc.—CONCLUDED.

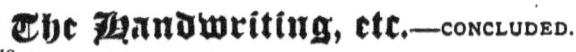

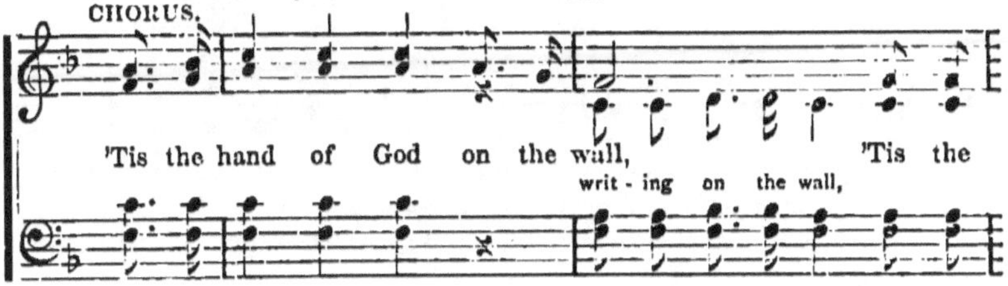
CHORUS.
'Tis the hand of God on the wall, 'Tis the
writ - ing on the wall,

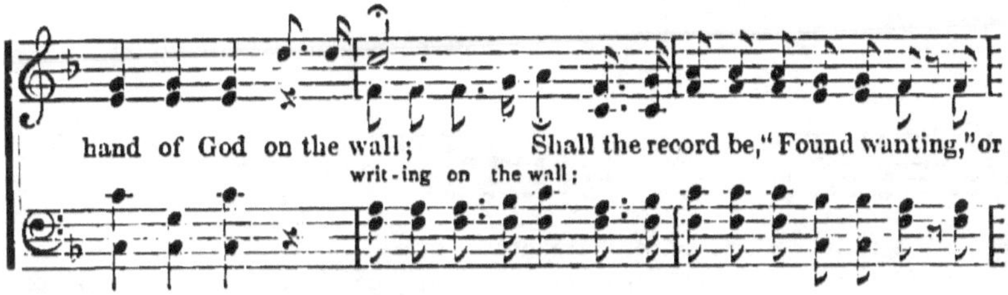
hand of God on the wall; Shall the record be, "Found wanting," or
writ - ing on the wall;

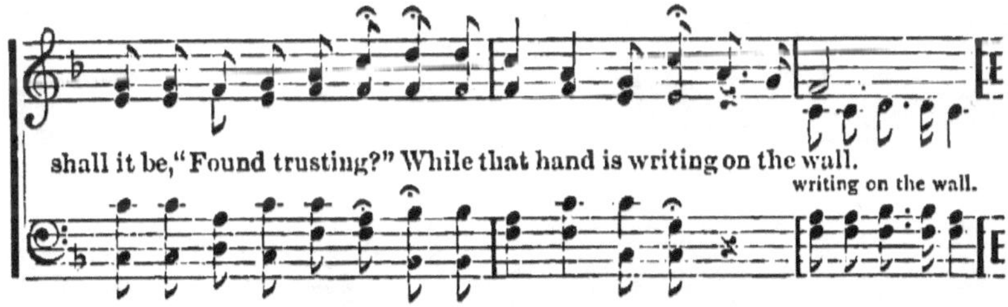
shall it be, "Found trusting?" While that hand is writing on the wall.
writing on the wall.

72 O for a Closer Walk.

C. WESLEY. Tune, ORTONVILLE.

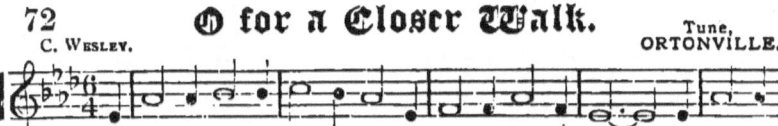

1. O for a closer walk with God, A calm and heavenly frame; A light to
2. Where is the blessedness I knew, When first I saw the Lord? Where is the

shine upon the road That leads me to the Lamb! That leads me to the Lamb!
soul-refreshing view Of Jesus and his word? Of Jesus and his word?

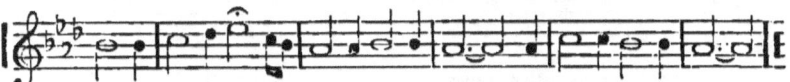

3 What peaceful hours I once enjoyed!
How sweet their memory still!
But they have left an aching void
The world can never fill.

4 Return, O holy Dove, return,
Sweet messenger of rest!
I hate the sins that made thee mourn,
And drove thee from my breast.

5 The dearest idol I have known,
Whate'er that idol be,
Help me to tear it from thy throne,
And worship only thee.

6 So shall my walk be close with God,
Calm and serene my frame;
So purer light shall mark the road
That leads me to the Lamb.

80. Follow Thou Me.

ARTHUR T. PIERSON, D. D.   JNO. R. SWENEY.

1. Follow thou me, says a gentle voice, Be my commands your highest choice;
2. Follow thou me is the Master's word, Hast thou the gentle message heard?
3. Follow thou me and take up thy cross, And for his sake count all things loss;
4. Follow thou me; if for good or ill, Choose thou the blessed Master's will;

Follow my footsteps, they will guide To the home where I a - bide.
Lo. he now waits to hear thee say, If thou wilt his words o - bey,—
Follow him now! why shouldst thou stray From thy God another day?
Close in his footsteps fearless tread, Blest the soul by Je - sus led.

CHORUS.

It is I say-ing, Follow thou me, Follow thou me, Follow thou me; No more delay-ing, Straightway obeying, Fol - low thou me!

5 Follow thou me! though obscure the way,
Upward it leads to endless day;
He who with Christ the cross will bear
Shall his crown in glory share.

6 Follow thou me: then shalt thou be
From every sin and stain made free;
Till thou shalt reach the home above,
Dwell with him in perfect love.

Copyright, 1886, by JOHN J. HOOD.

Bread and to Spare.—CONCLUDED.

bread and to spare, The house of my Father has bread and to spare.
bread, has bread and to spare,

82 The Lord of Life.

Mrs. Wm. Fawcett. Dr. H. L. Gilmour.

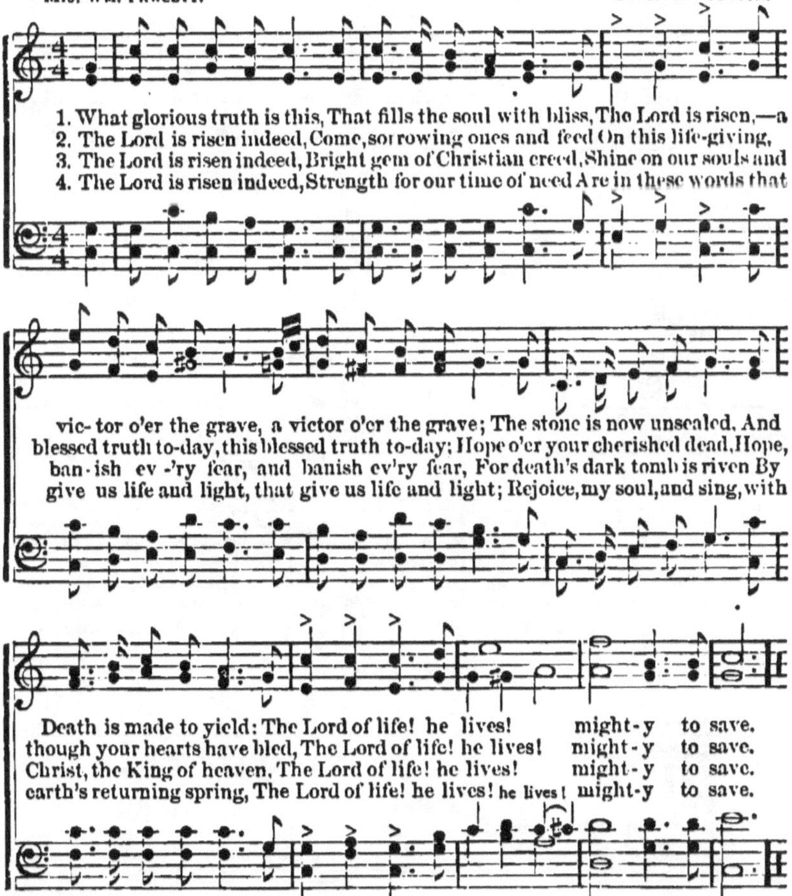

1. What glorious truth is this, That fills the soul with bliss, The Lord is risen,—a vic-tor o'er the grave, a victor o'er the grave; The stone is now unsealed, And Death is made to yield: The Lord of life! he lives! might-y to save.
2. The Lord is risen indeed, Come, sorrowing ones and feed On this life-giving, blessed truth to-day, this blessed truth to-day; Hope o'er your cherished dead, Hope though your hearts have bled, The Lord of life! he lives! might-y to save.
3. The Lord is risen indeed, Bright gem of Christian creed, Shine on our souls and ban-ish ev-'ry fear, and banish ev'ry fear, For death's dark tomb is riven By Christ, the King of heaven, The Lord of life! he lives! might-y to save.
4. The Lord is risen indeed, Strength for our time of need Are in these words that give us life and light, that give us life and light; Rejoice, my soul, and sing, with earth's returning spring, The Lord of life! he lives! he lives! might-y to save.

Copyright, 1896, by John J. Hood.

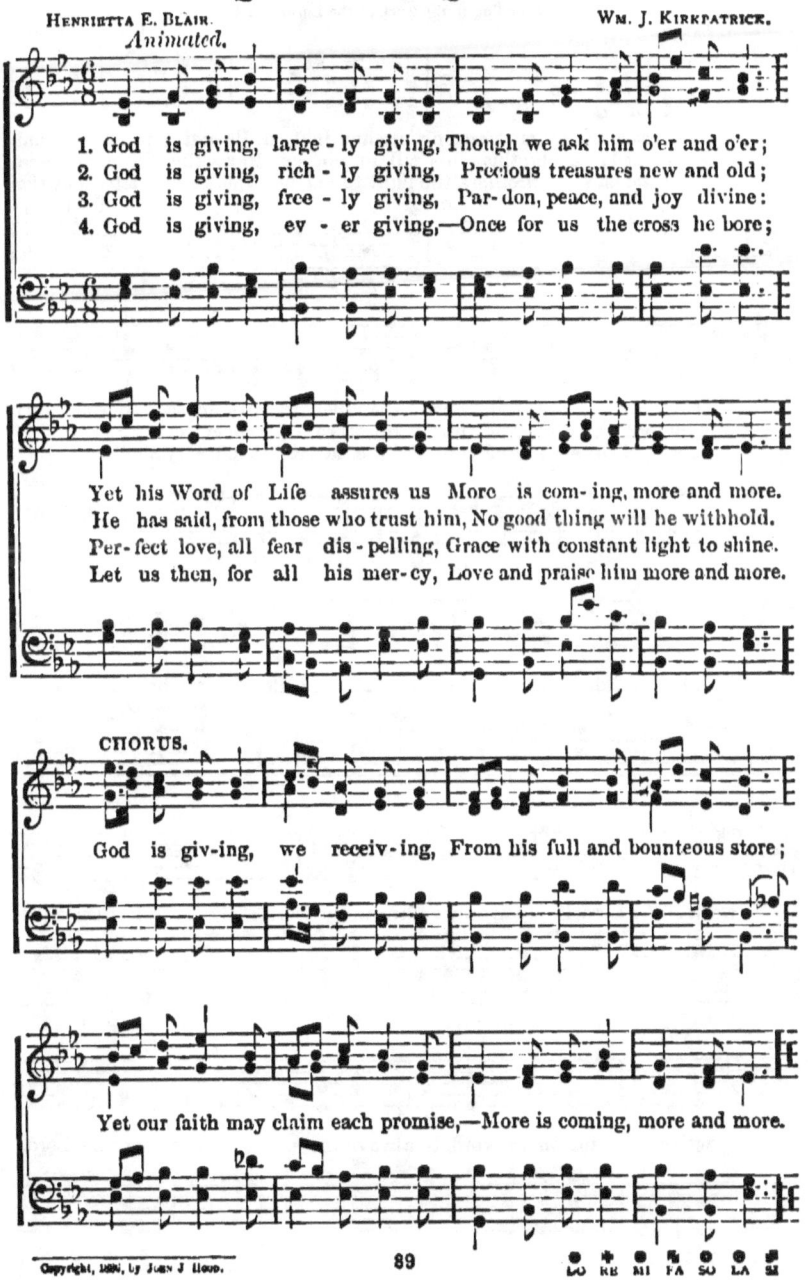

88 Songs in the calm, still Night.

JENNIE GARNETT. JNO. R. SWENEY.

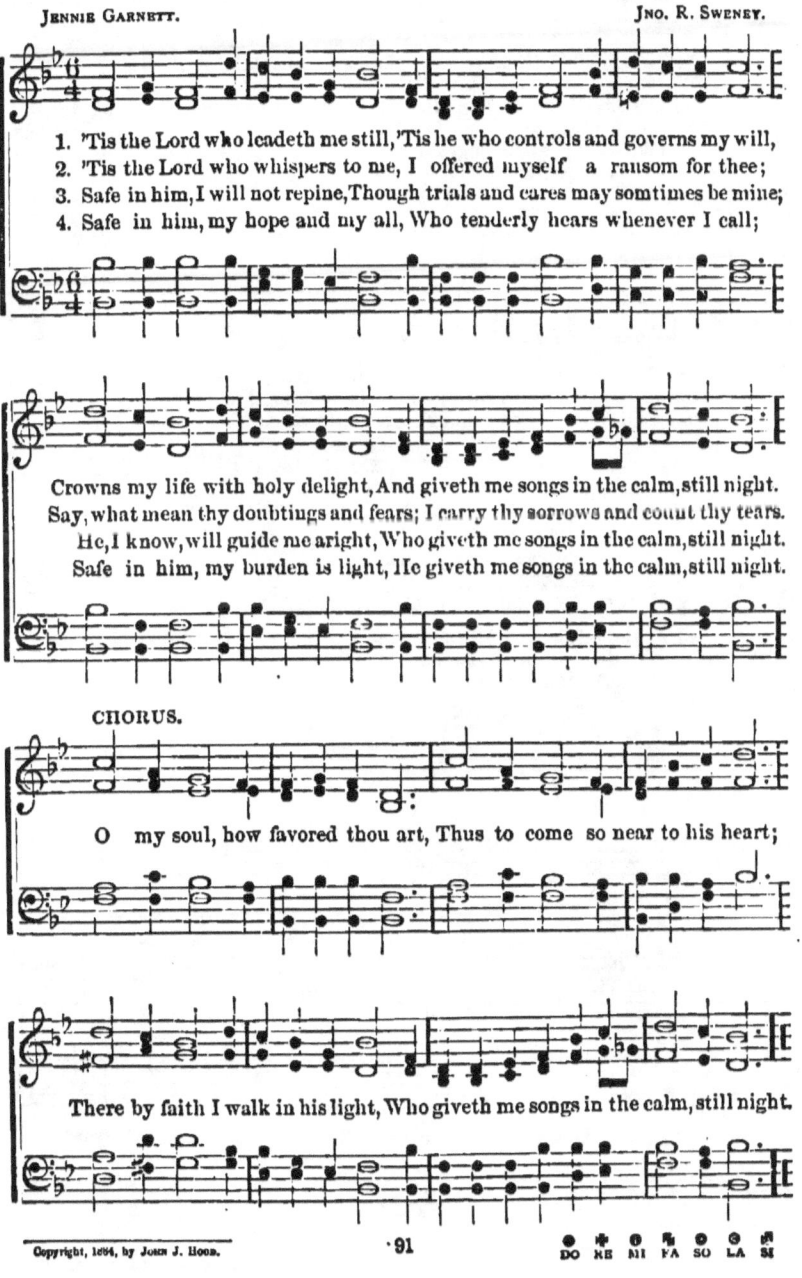

1. 'Tis the Lord who leadeth me still, 'Tis he who controls and governs my will,
2. 'Tis the Lord who whispers to me, I offered myself a ransom for thee;
3. Safe in him, I will not repine, Though trials and cares may sometimes be mine;
4. Safe in him, my hope and my all, Who tenderly hears whenever I call;

Crowns my life with holy delight, And giveth me songs in the calm, still night.
Say, what mean thy doubtings and fears; I carry thy sorrows and count thy tears.
He, I know, will guide me aright, Who giveth me songs in the calm, still night.
Safe in him, my burden is light, He giveth me songs in the calm, still night.

CHORUS.

O my soul, how favored thou art, Thus to come so near to his heart;

There by faith I walk in his light, Who giveth me songs in the calm, still night.

Copyright, 1884, by JOHN J. HOOD.

90. Are you ready for His coming?

T. ALCLIFFE TESKE. A. M. WORTMAN. M. D.

3. He will come in all his glory bright,
   As upon the mount he stood;
   Can you sing the glad hosanna loud,
   I am washed in Jesus blood?

4. Oh, the day draws nearer, nearer still,
   When the saints he will redeem;
   Now the light of morn is breaking fast,
   We can see its golden beam.

5. Yes, we're ready for his coming now
   And we watch, and wait, and pray,
   For the day to dawn in glory bright,
   And the night to roll away.

6. We are ready should he come for us,
   Ready now in peace to go;
   We are watching, and we're waiting still,
   With our robes as white as snow.

Copyright, 1885, by JOHN J. HOOD.

Look Aloft.—CONCLUDED.

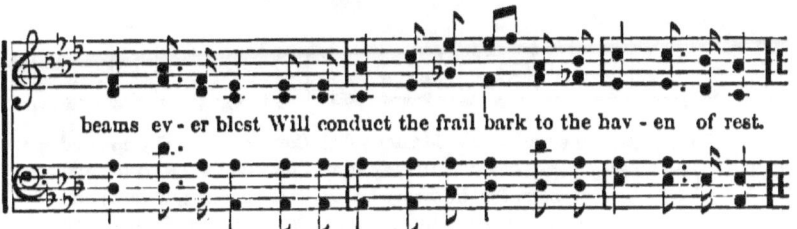

beams ev-er blest Will conduct the frail bark to the hav-en of rest.

92 Gentle Shepherd, Save Me Now.

Henrietta E. Blair. Wm. J. Kirkpatrick.

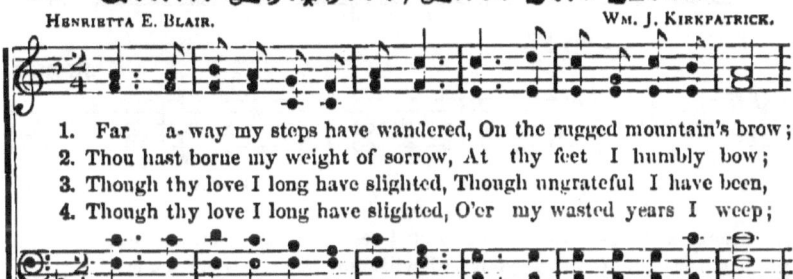

1. Far a-way my steps have wandered, On the rugged mountain's brow;
2. Thou hast borne my weight of sorrow, At thy feet I humbly bow;
3. Though thy love I long have slighted, Though ungrateful I have been,
4. Though thy love I long have slighted, O'er my wasted years I weep;

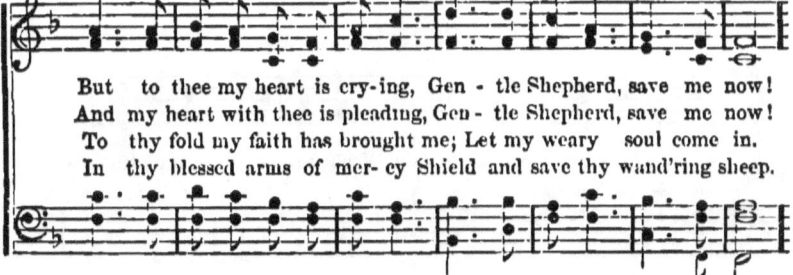

But to thee my heart is cry-ing, Gen-tle Shepherd, save me now!
And my heart with thee is pleading, Gen-tle Shepherd, save me now!
To thy fold my faith has brought me; Let my weary soul come in.
In thy blessed arms of mer-cy Shield and save thy wand'ring sheep.

D.S.—Un-to thee my heart is cry-ing, Gen-tle Shepherd, save me now!

CHORUS. D.S.

Save me now! save me now! Gen-tle Shepherd, save me now!

Every Day.—CONCLUDED.

greatest good aspire, From the high, still rising higher, Ev'ry day, ev'ry day.

100. Jesus, I come to Thee.

FANNY J. CROSBY.   WM. J KIRKPATRICK.

1. Je-sus, I come to thee, Long-ing for rest; Fold thou thy
2. Je-sus, I come to thee, Hear thou my cry; Save, or I
3. Now let the rolling waves Bend to thy will, Say to the
4. Swift-ly the part-ing clouds Fade from my sight; Yon-der thy

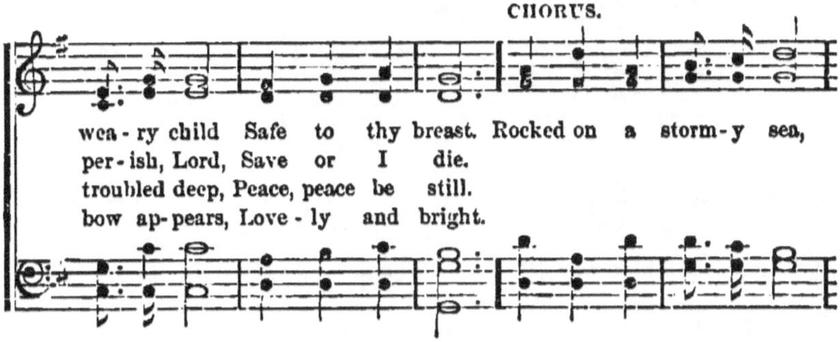

CHORUS.

wea-ry child Safe to thy breast. Rocked on a storm-y sea,
per-ish, Lord, Save or I die.
troubled deep, Peace, peace be still.
bow ap-pears, Love-ly and bright.

Oh, be not far from me. Lord, let me cling to thee, On-ly to thee.

Copyright, 1884, by John J. Hood.

Christ Shall Reign.—CONCLUDED.

104 Lr. Edwards. **Christmas Carol.—Hope's Bright Star.** Tune above.

1 Hail, hail, hail, beautiful sky, beautiful
  sky,
 Yonder comes the queen of morning,
  Night is gliding by;
 Over the world once more, folding her
  wings, folding her wings,
 Peace, her gentle harp awaking,
  Smiles and sings.
 Sweet as when the joyful tidings
 ||: Sounded long ago, :|| [them
 Sweet as when the shepherds heard
 ||: Still their numbers flow, :||
 Unto us is born a Saviour,
  He is born to-day;
 Come, behold the meek and lowly,
  Come quickly away.

Chorus.—
 Hail, hail, hail, beautiful light, beautiful
  Thro' the birth of our Redeemer [light,
  Making all so bright;   [ing afar,
 Beautiful light of God, shining afar, shin-
 Every eye may see its glory,
  Hope's bright star.

2 Come, come, come, tripping along trip-
 Carol o'er the sacred story [ping along,
  All have loved so long;
 List to the chiming bells, merry and clear,
   merry and clear,
 Happy Christmas, happy Christmas,
  Welcome, welcome here.
 Graceful boughs of green are waving,
 ||: Hearts with rapture beat, :||
 Love and mercy bending o'er us
 ||: Precious words repeat, :||
 Where the royal Prince of glory
  In a manger lay,
 Faith will lead and gently guide us,
  Come quickly away.

From "Hood's Carols for—(107)—Christmas, No. 6," by per.

105. Praise the Lord.

R. L. By per.   "All thy works shall praise thee, O Lord."—Ps. cxlv. 10.   Rev R. Lowry.

1. Lift the voice in ho-ly song, Awake, ye saints who love the Lord; Gath-er now in happy throng, And praise his name with one ac-cord;
2. Crowd his courts with loft-y praise, And sing the works that he hath done; Songs of love and honor raise To Christ the Lord, the e-qual Son;

Ye who know the great sal-va-tion, Sing the triumphs of his grace,
Shout a-loud, ye souls in glo-ry; Swell the song, ye saints be-low;
And with highest ad-o-ra-tion, Come be-fore Je-ho-vah's face.
Till the heav'ns shall tell the sto-ry, And the earth the strain shall know.

Copyright, 1875, by Biglow & Main.

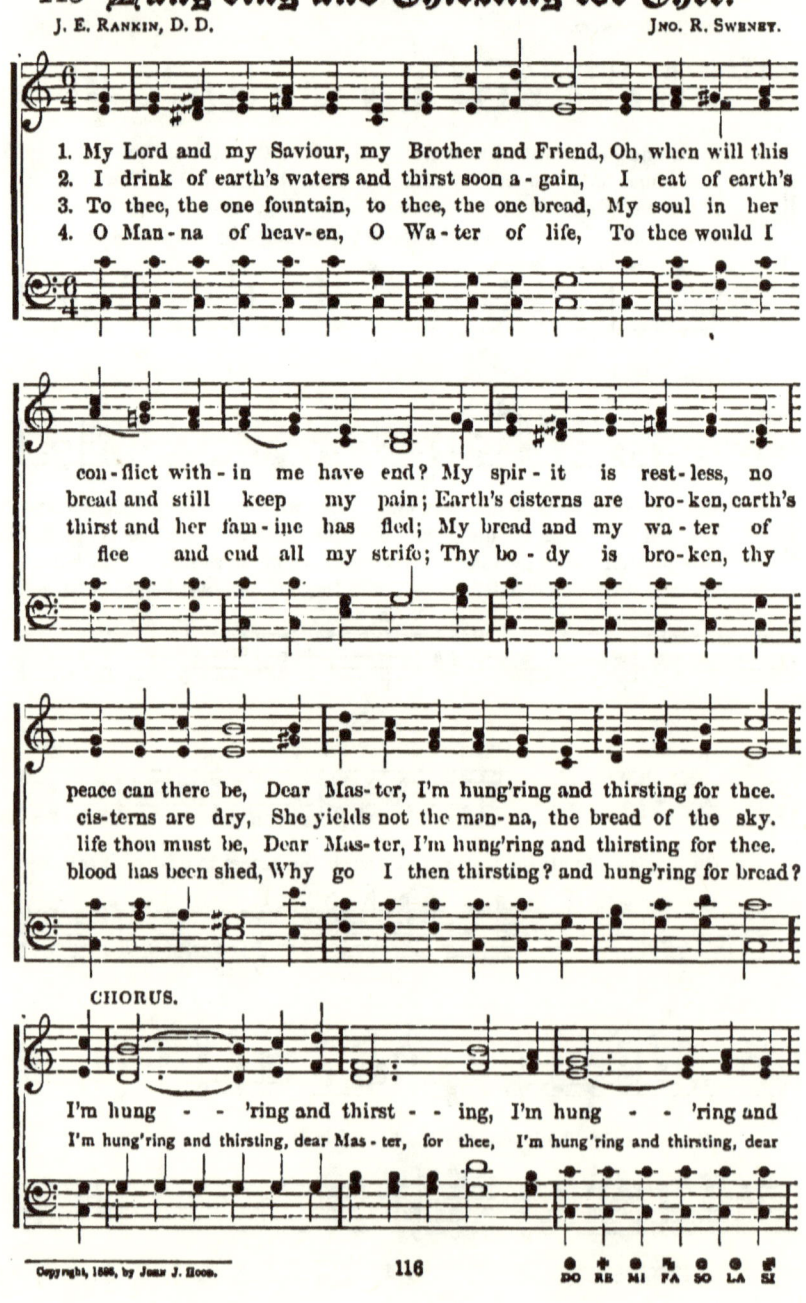

Hung'ring and Thirsting, etc.—CONCLUDED.

My Redeemer.

P. P. Bliss. "O Lord, my strength, and my redeemer."—Ps. xix. 14. James McGranahan.

By per. of The John Church Co., owners of copyright.

DO RE MI FA SO LA SI

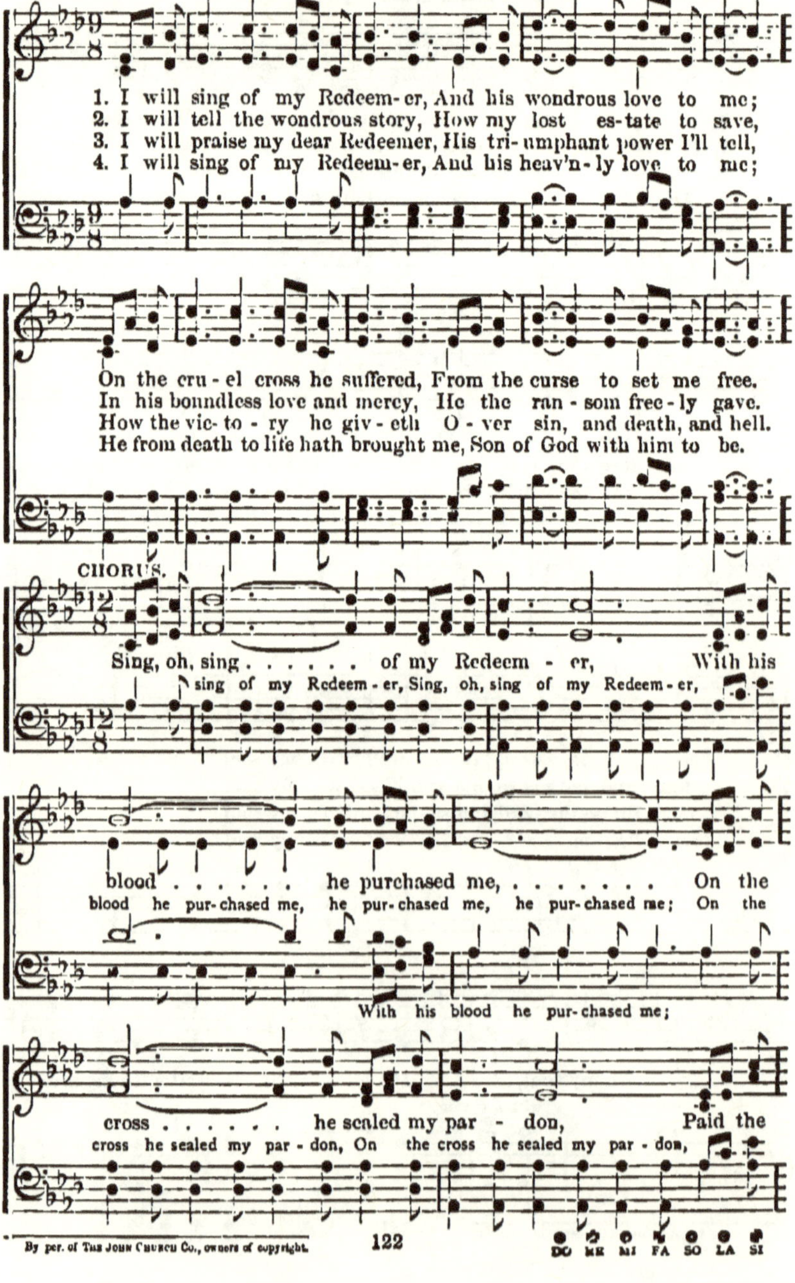

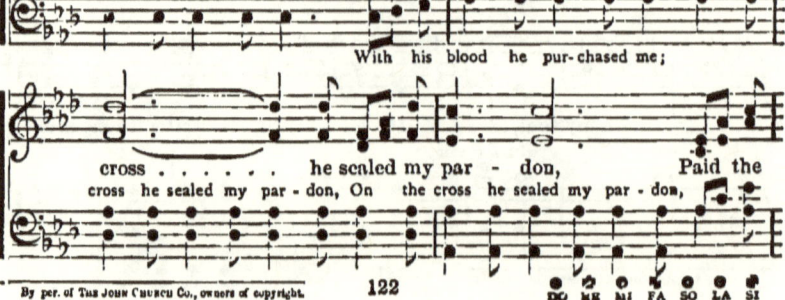

My Redeemer.—CONCLUDED.

119. O Receive Him.

LIZZIE EDWARDS.   FOR PRIMARY CLASS.   JNO. R. SWENEY.

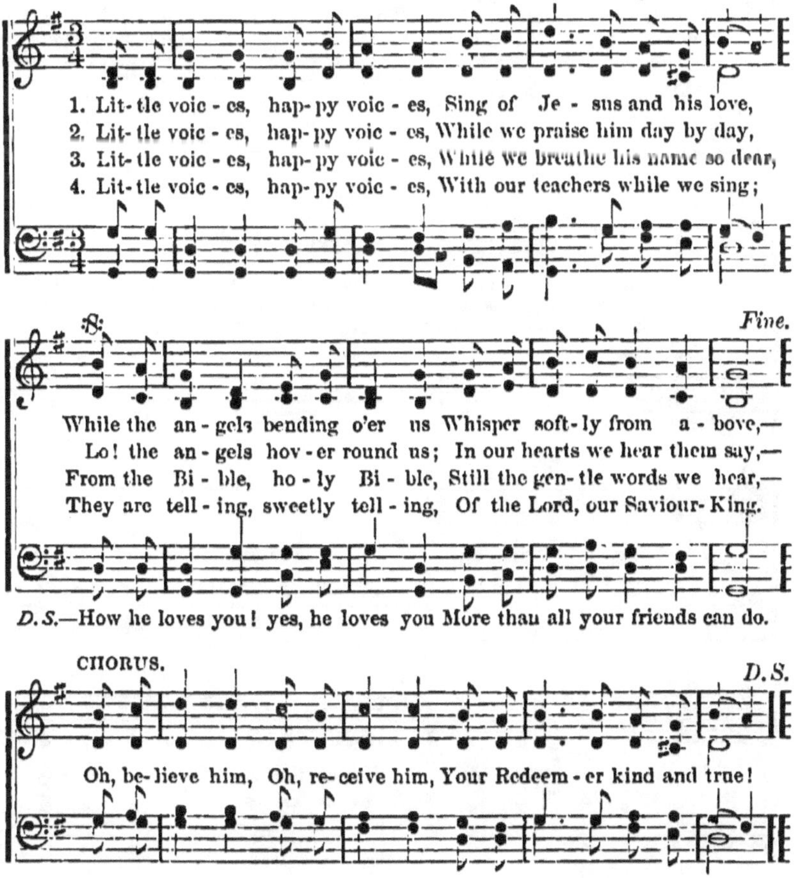

1. Lit-tle voic-es, hap-py voic-es, Sing of Jesus and his love,
2. Lit-tle voic-es, hap-py voic-es, While we praise him day by day,
3. Lit-tle voic-es, hap-py voic-es, While we breathe his name so dear,
4. Lit-tle voic-es, hap-py voic-es, With our teachers while we sing;

While the an-gels bending o'er us Whisper soft-ly from a-bove,—
Lo! the an-gels hov-er round us; In our hearts we hear them say,—
From the Bi-ble, ho-ly Bi-ble, Still the gen-tle words we hear,—
They are tell-ing, sweetly tell-ing, Of the Lord, our Saviour-King.

D.S.—How he loves you! yes, he loves you More than all your friends can do.

CHORUS.   *D.S.*

Oh, be-lieve him, Oh, re-ceive him, Your Redeem-er kind and true!

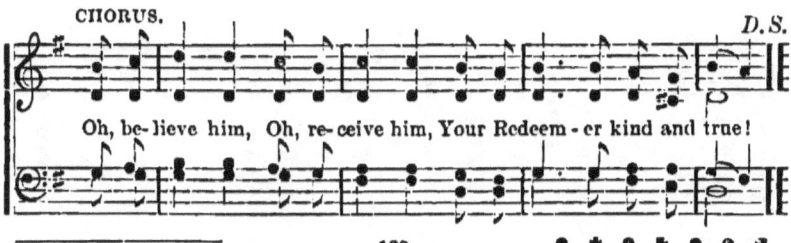

Oh, to be over Yonder.—CONCLUDED.

Oh, . . . to be o - ver yon - der, In . . . . that land of won-der,
Oh, to be o - - ver yon-der, yon-der, In that land, that land of wonder,

There . . . to be for-ev - er In the presence of the King.
There to be for - - ev - er

124 C. J. B. A Sinner like Me. CHAS. J. BUTLER.

1. I was once far away from the Saviour, And as vile as a sinner could be,
I wondered if Christ the Redeemer Could save a poor sinner like me.

2 I wandered on in the darkness,
 Not a ray of light could I see,
And the thought filled my heart with sad-
 There's no hope for a sinner like me. [ness,

3 I then fully trusted in Jesus,
 And oh, what a joy came to me;
My heart was filled with his praises,
 For saving a sinner like me.

4 No longer in darkness I'm walking,
 For the light is now shining on me,
And now unto others I'm telling,
 How he saved a poor sinner like me.

5 And when life's journey is over,
 And I the dear Saviour shall see,
I'll praise him for ever and ever,
 For saving a sinner like me.

Copyright, 1881, by JOHN J. HOOD.   OJW-I

126. THEO. MONOD. **Forward, March.** WM. J. KIRKPATRICK.

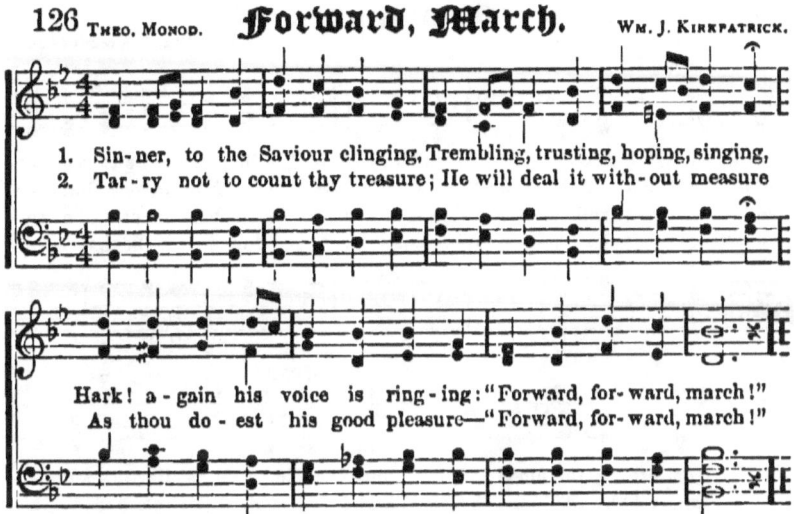

1. Sinner, to the Saviour clinging, Trembling, trusting, hoping, singing,
2. Tarry not to count thy treasure; He will deal it without measure

Hark! again his voice is ringing: "Forward, forward, march!"
As thou doest his good pleasure—"Forward, forward, march!"

3 Art thou faint? He stands beside thee;
He shall help thee, guard thee, guide thee;
In his shadow he shall hide thee—
"Forward, forward, march!"

4 Through th' allurements of temptation,
Through the fires of tribulation,
Holding forth the great salvation,
"Forward, forward, march!"

5 By ten thousand foes surrounded,
Mocked, opposed, assaulted, wounded,
Thou shalt never be confounded,
"Forward, forward, march!"

6 Till thy bending head be hoary,
Till shall close thine earthly story,
Till thou step from grace to glory,
"Forward, forward, march!"

Copyright, 1836, by JOHN J. HOOD.

127 **Victory.** 7s.

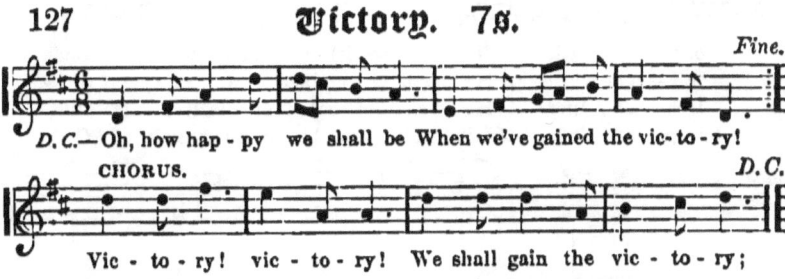

D.C.—Oh, how happy we shall be When we've gained the victory!

CHORUS.

Victory! victory! We shall gain the victory;

1 WHAT are these arrayed in white,
   Brighter than the noon-day sun?
   Foremost of the sons of light;
   Nearest the eternal throne?

2 These are they that bore the cross;
   Nobly for their Master stood;
   Sufferers in his righteous cause;
   Followers of the dying God.

3 Out of great distress they came;
   Washed their robes by faith below
   In the blood of yonder Lamb,
   Blood that washes white as snow:

4 Therefore are they next the throne;
   Serve their Maker day and night;
   God resides among his own;
   God doth in his saints delight.

5 He that on the throne doth reign,
   Them the Lamb shall always feed;
   With the tree of life sustain;
   To the living fountains lead;

6 He shall all their sorrows chase
   All their wants at once remove;
   Wipe the tears from every face;
   Fill up every soul with love.

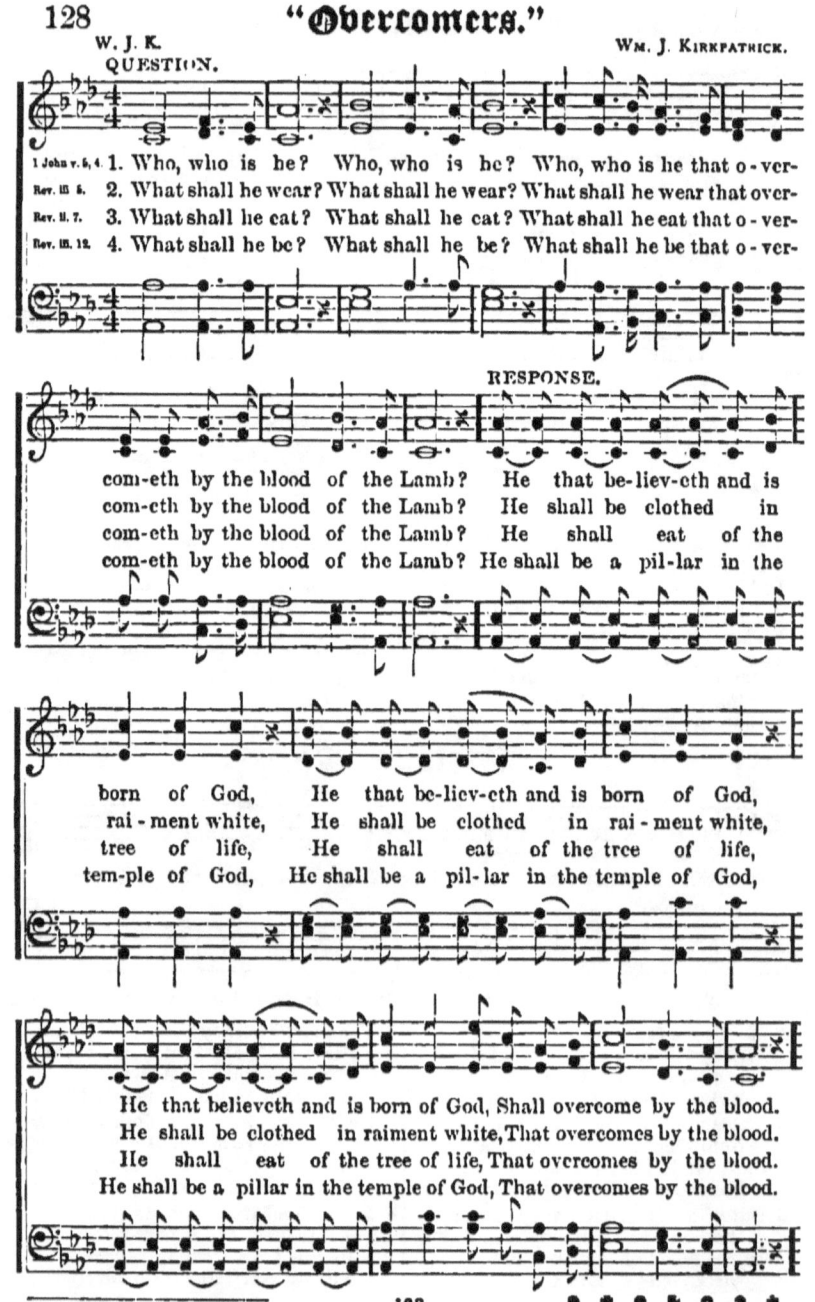

"Overcomers."—CONCLUDED.

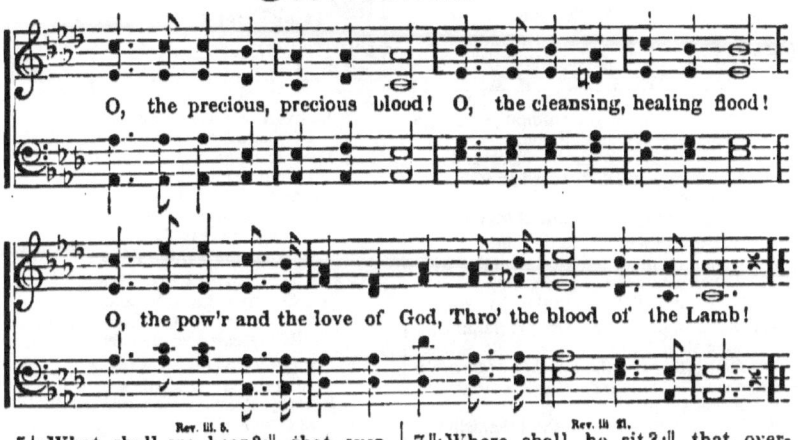

O, the precious, precious blood! O, the cleansing, healing flood!
O, the pow'r and the love of God, Thro' the blood of the Lamb!

Rev. iii. 5.
5 ‖:What shall we hear?:‖ that over-By the blood of the Lamb? [cometh
‖:He shall hear his name con-|fessed in heaven,:‖
That overcomes by the blood.

Rev. xxi. 7.
6 ‖:What shall he have?:‖ that over-By the blood of the Lamb? [cometh
‖:God will give him all things, and| make him his son,:‖
That overcomes by the blood.

Rev. iii. 21.
7 ‖:Where shall he sit?:‖ that over-By the blood of the Lamb? [cometh
‖:He shall sit with | Jesus, on his throne,:‖
That overcomes by the blood.

1 John v. 4
8 ‖:What is the victory?:‖ that over-By the blood of the Lamb? [cometh
‖:Faith is the victory that | overcometh, ‖:
By the blood of the Lamb.

129 All the way long it is Jesus.

1. { O good old way, how sweet thou art! All the way long it is Je-sus;
{ May none of us from thee de-part; All the way long it is Je-sus.

CHORUS.
Je-sus, Je-sus, Why, all the way long it is Je-sus.

2 But may our actions always say
We're marching in the good old way.

3 This note above the rest shall swell,
That Jesus doeth all things well.

130 What a Gathering.

1 AT the sounding of the trumpet, when the
    saints are gathered home,
We will greet each other by the crystal sea,
With the friends and all the loved ones there a-
    waiting us to come,
What a gathering of the faithful that will be!

Cho.—What a gathering, gathering,
   At the sounding of the glorious jubilee!
   What a gathering, gathering,
   What a gathering of the faithful that will be!

2 When the angel of the Lord proclaims that
    time shall be no more,   [see,
We shall gather, and the saved and ransom'd
Then to meet again together, on the bright ce-
    lestial shore,
What a gathering of the faithful that will be!

3 At the great and final judgment when the hid-
    den comes to light,
When the Lord in all his glory we shall see,
At the bidding of our Saviour, "Come, ye bless-
    ed, to my right,".
What a gathering of the faithful that will be!

4 When the golden harps are sounding, and the
    angel bands proclaim,
In triumphant strains, the glorious jubilee,
Then to meet and join to sing the song of Moses
    and the Lamb,
What a gathering of the faithful that will be!

131 The New Song.

1 There are songs of joy that I loved to sing
When my heart was as blithe as a bird in spring;
But the song I have learned is so full of cheer,
That the dawn shines out in the darkness drear.

Cho.—O, the new, new song! :||
I can sing it now with the ransomed throng;
Power and dominion to him that shall reign,
Glory and praise to the Lamb that was slain.

2 There are strains of home that are dear as life,
And I list to them oft 'mid the din of strife:
But I know of a home that is wondrous fair,
And I sing the psalm they are singing there.

3 Can my lips be mute, or my heart be sad,
When the gracious Master hath made me glad?
When he points where the many mansions be,
And sweetly says, "There is one for thee"?

4 I shall catch the gleam of its jasper wall
When I come to the gloom of the evenfall,
For I know that the shadows, dreary and dim,
Have a path of light that will lead to him.

132 Is my Name written There?

1 LORD, I care not for riches,
   Neither silver nor gold;
I would make sure of heaven,
   I would enter the fold.
In the book of thy kingdom,
   With its pages so fair,
Tell me, Jesus my Saviour,
   Is my name written there?

Cho.—Is my name written there,
   On the page white and fair?
In the book of thy kingdom,
   Is my name written there?

2 Lord, my sins they are many,
   Like the sands of the sea,
But thy blood, O my Saviour,
   Is sufficient for me;
For thy promise is written,
   In bright letters that glow,
"Though your sins be as scarlet,
   I will make them like snow."

3 Oh! that beautiful city,
   With its mansions of light,
With its glorified beings,
   In pure garments of white;
Where no evil thing cometh
   To despoil what is fair;
Where the angels are watching,—
   Is my name written there?

133 The New Name.

1 WE shall have a new name in that land,
In that land, that sunny, sunny land,
When we meet the bright angelic band,
   In that sunny land.   [there;
A new name, a new name we'll receive up
A new name, a new name, all who enter there.

Cho.—We shall have a new name in that land,
In that land, that sunny, sunny land,
When we meet the bright angelic band,
   In that sunny land.

2 We'll receive it in a pure, white stone,
And no one will know the name therein;
Only unto him who hath 'tis known,
   When we're free from sin.   [there;
A white stone, a white stone we'll receive up
A white stone, a white stone, all who enter there.

3 Don't you wonder what that name will be,
Sweeter far than aught on earth can be,
We will be quite satisfied when we
   Shall that new name know.
I wonder, I wonder what that name will be,
I wonder, I wonder, what he'll give to me.

134. Draw me to Thee.

"And I will cause him to draw near, and he shall approach unto me."
Jer. xxx. 21.

M. A. W. Cook. E. S. Lorenz.

1. Lord, weak and im-po-tent I stand, As fettered by an unseen hand;
2. In vain I strug-gle to be free; I would, but cannot, fly to thee;
3. Oh, bring me near-er, near-er still, That thine own peace my soul may fill,
4. Here, Lord, I would for-ev-er bide, And nev-er wan-der from thy side;

Break thou the strong and sub-tle band, And draw me close to thee.
Ope thou the pris-on door for me, And draw me close to thee.
And I may rest in thy sweet will; Lord, draw me close to thee.
Beneath thy wing do thou me hide, And draw me close to thee.

D. S.—Beneath thy wing do thou me hide, And draw me close to thee.

CHORUS.

Draw me close to thee, Sav-iour, Draw me close to thee;
close to thee, Sav-iour,

By permission.

135. For me, for me.

1. { Jesus shed his precious blood, For me, for me;
   { Jesus brings me back to God, ... Jesus saves me now.

2 There for me the Saviour stands,
Shows his wounds and spreads his hands.

3 God is love, I know, I feel,
Jesus lives and loves me still.

4 Plenteous grace with thee is found,
Let the healing showers abound.

5 Rock of ages cleft for me,
Now I hide myself in thee.

136. Stand at Your Post.

Lizzie Edwards.   Jno. R. Swenky.

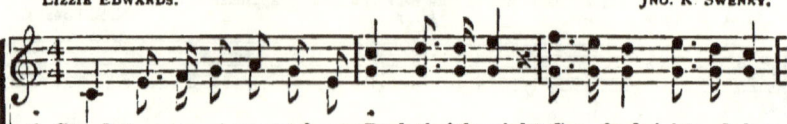

1. Stand at your post, ye watchmen, Dark tho' the night; See afar, bright and clear,
2. Stand at your post of du-ty, Be not dismayed, Christ the Lord rideth on
3. Stand at your post of du-ty, Truth must prevail, Joyful news, welcome news,
4. Stand at your post of duty, Cheer, watchmen, cheer; Lo, the time, promised time,

Dawns the morning light; Sound, sound the trump of Zion O'er land and sea;
Now in strength arrayed; Lift up the gos-pel banner, Watchmen, proclaim
Comes with ev'ry gale; Lo! at the feet of Jesus Proud monarchs fall;
Now is drawing near; Bright o'er the distant mountain On rolls the day,

CHORUS.

Tell a-gain the happy tidings, Grace is free.   Bright   Star   of   the
Peace and life to ev-'ry creature Thro' his name.
They have heard the gospel message, Joy to all.
Driving ev-'ry mist and shadow Far a-way.   Bright, bright Star,

morn - ing, Thou bles-sed Star of glo - ry, bles-sed Star of glo - ry,
bright, bright Star,

Copyright, 1886, by John J. Hood.

DO RE MI FA SO LA SI

Stand at Your Post.—CONCLUDED.

137

3 Anxious no longer for self,
    Shrinking no longer from pain;
  Leaning on Jesus alone,
    He all my care will sustain.
      Leaning on Jesus, etc.

4 Leaning, I walk in "The Way,"
    Leaning, "The Truth" I shall know;
  Leaning on heart-throbs of Christ,
    Safe into "Life" I may go.
      Leaning on Jesus, etc.

From " Leaflet Gems, No. 2," by per.

142 Come to Jesus.

1 COME to Jesus, come to Jesus,
  Come to Jesus just now,
Just now come to Jesus,
  Come to Jesus just now.

2 He will save you.
3 Oh, believe him.
4 He is able.
5 He is willing.
6 He'll receive you.
7 Flee to Jesus.
8 Call unto him.
9 He will hear you.
10 He'll have mercy.
11 He'll forgive you.
12 He will cleanse you.
13 He'll renew you.
14 He will clothe you.
15 Jesus loves you.

143 Fill me now.

1 HOVER o'er me, Holy Spirit;
  Bathe my trembling heart and brow;
  Fill me with thy hallowed presence,
  Come, oh, come and fill me now.

Cho.—Fill me now, fill me now,
  Jesus, come and fill me now,
  Fill me with thy hallowed presence,—
  Come, oh, come and fill me now.

2 Thou canst fill me, gracious Spirit,
  Though I cannot tell thee how;
  But I need thee, greatly need thee;
  Come, oh, come and fill me now.

3 I am weakness, full of weakness;
  At thy sacred feet I bow;
  Blest, divine, eternal Spirit,
  Fill with pow'r, and fill me now.

4 Cleanse and comfort; bless and save me;
  Bathe, oh, bathe my heart and brow;
  Thou art comforting and saving,
  Thou art sweetly filling now.

144 The Child of a King.

1 MY Father is rich in houses and lands,
He holdeth the wealth of the world in his hands!
Of rubies and diamonds, of silver and gold
His coffers are full,—he has riches untold.

Cho.—I'm the child of a King,
  The child of a King;
    With Jesus my Saviour
  I'm the child of a King.

2 My Father's own Son, the Saviour of men;
Once wandered o'er earth as the poorest of them,
But now he is reigning forever on high, [down,—
And will give me a home in heaven by and by.

3 I once was an outcast stranger on earth,
A sinner by choice, an alien by birth! [down,—
But I've been adopted, my name's written
An heir to a mansion, a robe, and a crown.

4 A tent or a cottage, why should I care?
They're building a palace for me over there!
Though exiled from home, yet still I may sing:
All glory to God, I'm the child of a King.

145 The Rock that is Higher.

1 OH, sometimes the shadows are deep,
  And rough seems the path to the goal,
And sorrows, sometimes how they sweep
  Like tempests down over the soul.

Cho.—Oh, then to the rock let me fly,
  To the rock that is higher than I. :||

2 Oh, sometimes how long seems the day,
  And sometimes how weary my feet;
But toiling in life's dusty way,
  The Rock's blessed shadow, how sweet!

3 Oh, near to the Rock let me keep,
  Or blessings or sorrows prevail;
Or climbing the mountain-way steep,
  Or walking the shadowy vale.

146 Bringing in the Sheaves.

1 Sowing in the morning, sowing seeds of kindness,
Sowing in the noon-tide, and the dewy eves;
Waiting for the harvest, and the time of reaping,
  We shall come rejoicing, bringing in the sheaves.

Cho.—Bringing in the sheaves, bringing in the
  sheaves, [sheaves. :||
  We shall come rejoicing, bringing in the

2 Sowing in the sunshine, sowing in the shadows, [breeze;
Fearing neither clouds nor winter's chilling
By and by the harvest, and the labor ended,
  We shall come rejoicing, bringing in the sheaves.

3 Go, then, ever weeping, sowing for the Master,
  Though the loss sustained our spirit often grieves;
When our weeping's over he will bid us welcome, [sheaves.
  We shall come rejoicing, bringing in the

147. O Prodigal, Don't Stay Away.

J. E. RANKIN, D. D.   "I will arise and go unto my Father."—Luke xv. 18.   J. W. BISCHOFF.

1. O prod-i-gal, don't stay away! The Fa-ther is waiting to-day; There's room and to spare, There is raiment to wear, O prod-igal, don't stay a-way.
2. O prodigal brother, come home! Why longer in wretchedness roam? You're lone-ly and lost, You are driven and toss'd, O prod-igal brother, come home.
3. O prodigal, what will you do? Love's ta-ble is wait-ing for you; For-giveness so sweet, Sure, your coming will greet, O prodigal, what will you do?
4. O prod-i-gal brother, a-rise! For pardon, look up to the skies; No longer then stray From thy Father away, O prod-i-gal brother, a-rise.

CHORUS.

Will you come? Will you come? Will you come, come home to-day? There is welcome for you, There's a kiss, kind and true, Then, O prodigal, don't stay away.

Will you come?   Will you come?   Will you come?

From "Gospel Bells," by per.

149. Cast thy Burden on the Lord.

"Casting all your care upon him, for he careth for you."
1 Peter v. 7.

W. J. K.   WM. J. KIRKPATRICK.

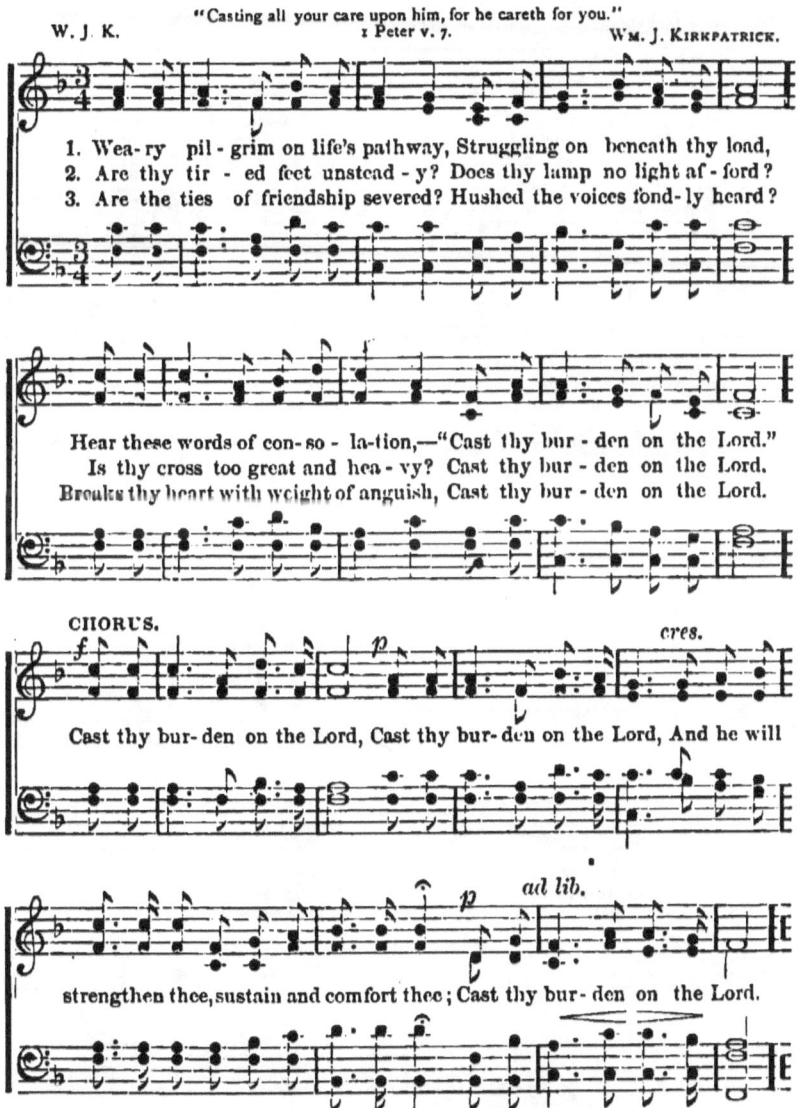

1. Weary pilgrim on life's pathway, Struggling on beneath thy load,
2. Are thy tired feet unsteady? Does thy lamp no light afford?
3. Are the ties of friendship severed? Hushed the voices fondly heard?

Hear these words of consolation,—"Cast thy burden on the Lord."
Is thy cross too great and heavy? Cast thy burden on the Lord.
Breaks thy heart with weight of anguish, Cast thy burden on the Lord.

CHORUS.

Cast thy burden on the Lord, Cast thy burden on the Lord, And he will strengthen thee, sustain and comfort thee; Cast thy burden on the Lord.

4 Does thy heart with faintness falter?
Does thy mind forget his word?
Does thy strength succumb to weakness?
Cast thy burden on the Lord.

5 He will hold thee up from falling,
He will guide thy steps aright;
He will strengthen each endeavor;
He will keep thee by his might.

Copyright, 1880, by JOHN J. HOOD.   OJW-K

Ah! 'tis the old, old Story.—CONCLUDED.

Ah! 'tis the old, old stor-y, . . Tempted and led a-stray. .
Yes, 'tis the old, old stor-y, . . Full of a grace di-vine. .

151 Light after Darkness.

DUET. JNO. R. SWENEY.

1. Light af-ter darkness, Gain af-ter loss, Strength af-ter
2. Sheaves af-ter sow-ing, Sun af-ter rain, Sight af-ter
3. Near af-ter dis-tant, Gleam af-ter gloom, Love af-ter

weakness, Crown af-ter cross, Sweet af-ter bit-ter,
mys-tery, Peace af-ter pain, Joy af-ter sor-row,
loneliness, Life af-ter tomb; Af-ter long a-go-ny,

Song af-ter fears, Home af-ter wander-ing, Praise af-ter tears.
Calm af-ter blast, Rest af-ter weari-ness, Sweet rest at last.
Rap-ture of bliss; Right was the path-way Leading to this!

From "Goodly Pearls," by per.

DO RE MI FA SO LA SI

152 Sun of My Soul.

1 SUN of my soul, thou Saviour dear,
It is not night if thou be near;
Oh, may no earth-born cloud arise,
To hide thee from thy servant's eyes.

2 When the soft dews of kindly sleep
My wearied eye-lids gently steep,
Be my last thought, how sweet to rest
Forever on my Saviour's breast.

3 Abide with me from morn till eve,
For without thee I cannot live;
Abide with me when night is nigh,
For without thee I dare not die.

4 Watch by the sick: enrich the poor
With blessings from thy boundless store;
Be every mourner's sleep to-night,
Like infant's slumbers, pure and light.

153 Sing of His Mighty Love.

1 OH, bliss of the purified, bliss of the free,
I plunge in the crimson tide opened for me;
O'er sin and uncleanness exulting I stand,
And point to the print of the nails in his hand.

Cho.—Oh, sing of his mighty love,
 ‖: Sing of his mighty love, :‖
  Mighty to save.

2 Oh, bliss of the purified, Jesus is mine,
No longer in dread condemnation I pine;
In conscious salvation I sing of his grace,
Who lifteth upon me the light of his face.

3 Oh, bliss of the purified, bliss of the pure,
No wound hath the soul that his blood cannot
   cure; [rest,
No sorrow-bowed head but may sweetly find
No tears but may dry them on Jesus' breast.

4 O Jesus the crucified, thee will I sing,
My blessed Redeemer, my God and my King;
My soul filled with rapture shall shout o'er
   the grave,
And triumph in death in the "Mighty to Save."

154 Revive Thy Work.

1 WE praise thee, O God, for the Son of thy
     love,
For Jesus who died, and is now gone above.

Cho.—Hallelujah! thine the glory, hallelujah!
     amen;
Hallelujah! thine the glory, revive us again.

2 We praise thee, O God, for thy Spirit of light
Who has shown us our Saviour and scattered our night.

3 All glory and praise to the Lamb that was
     slain, [every stain.
Who has borne all our sins, and has cleansed

4 All glory and praise to the God of all grace,
Who has bought us, and sought us, and
     guided our ways.

5 Revive us again, fill each heart with thy love;
May each soul be rekindled with fire from
     above.

155 How Sweet the Name.

1 How sweet the name of Jesus sounds
In a believer's ear;
It soothes his sorrows, heals his wounds,
And drives away his fear.

2 It makes the wounded spirit whole,
And calms the troubled breast;
'Tis manna to the hungry soul,
And to the weary rest.

3 Jesus, my Shepherd, Saviour, Friend;
My Prophet, Priest, and King;
My Lord, my Life, my Way, my End,—
Accept the praise I bring.

4 I would thy boundless love proclaim
With every fleeting breath;
So shall the music of thy name
Refresh my soul in death.

156 Even Me.

1 LORD, I hear of showers of blessing
Thou art scattering full and free—
Showers the thirsty land refreshing;
Let some droppings fall on me.

Cho.—Even me, even me,
Let thy blessing fall on me.

2 Pass me not, O gracious Father!
Sinful though my heart may be;
Thou might'st leave me, but the rather
Let thy mercy fall on me.

3 Pass me not, O tender Saviour!
Let me love and cling to thee;
I am longing for thy favor;
Whilst thou'rt calling, oh, call me.

4 Pass me not, O mighty Spirit!
Thou can'st make the blind to see;
Witnesser of Jesus' merit,
Speak the word of power to me.

157. Wont You Love My Jesus?

SALLIE SMITH. JNO. R. SWENEY.

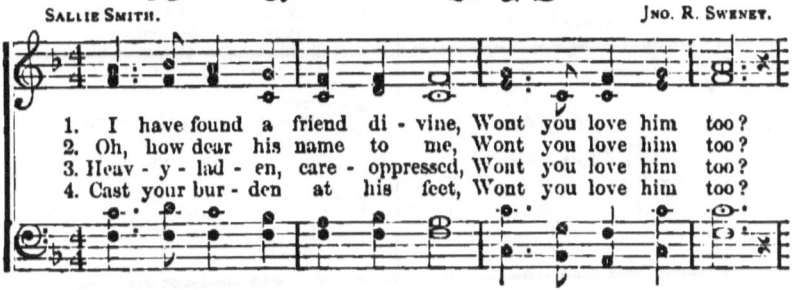

1. I have found a friend di-vine, Wont you love him too?
2. Oh, how dear his name to me, Wont you love him too?
3. Heav-y-lad-en, care-oppressed, Wont you love him too?
4. Cast your bur-den at his feet, Wont you love him too?

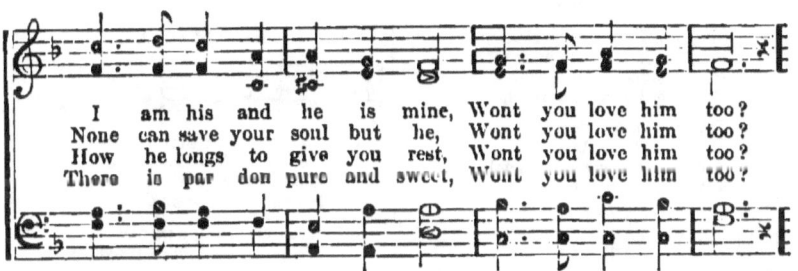

I am his and he is mine, Wont you love him too?
None can save your soul but he, Wont you love him too?
How he longs to give you rest, Wont you love him too?
There is par-don pure and sweet, Wont you love him too?

CHORUS.

Wont you love my Je-sus, My pre-cious, precious Je-sus?

Wont you love my Je-sus? He is waiting now for you.

Copyright, 1884, by JOHN J. HOOD.

FAMILIAR HYMNS.

158. Trusting Jesus, that is all.

1 SIMPLY trusting every day;
   Trusting, though a stormy way;
   Even when my faith is small,
   Trusting Jesus, that is all.

Cho.—Trusting him while life shall last,
   Trusting him till earth is past,—
   Till within the jasper wall—
   Trusting Jesus, that is all.

2 Brightly doth his Spirit shine
   Into this poor heart of mine;
   While he leads, I cannot fall,
   Trusting Jesus, that is all.

3 Singing, if my way is clear;
   Praying, if the path is drear;
   If in danger, for him call—
   Trusting Jesus, that is all.

4 Trusting as the moments fly,
   Trusting as the days go by,
   Trusting him whate'er befall—
   Trusting Jesus, that is all.

159. Fountain.

1 THERE is a fountain filled with blood
   Drawn from Immanuel's veins;
   And sinners, plunged beneath that flood,
   Lose all their guilty stains.

2 The dying thief rejoiced to see
   That fountain in his day;
   And there may I, though vile as he,
   Wash all my sins away.

3 Thou dying Lamb! thy precious blood
   Shall never lose its power,
   Till all the ransomed Church of God
   Are saved, to sin no more.

4 E'er since, by faith, I saw the stream
   Thy flowing wounds supply,
   Redeeming love has been my theme,
   And shall be till I die.

160. Coronation.

1 ALL hail the power of Jesus' name!
   Let angels prostrate fall;
   Bring forth the royal diadem,
   And crown him Lord of all.

2 Ye chosen seed of Israel's race,
   Ye ransomed from the fall,
   Hail him who saves you by his grace,
   And crown him Lord of all.

3 Sinners, whose love can ne'er forget
   The wormwood and the gall;
   Go, spread your trophies at his feet,
   And crown him Lord of all.

4 Let every kindred, every tribe,
   On this terrestrial ball,
   To him all majesty ascribe,
   And crown him Lord of all.

5 O that with yonder sacred throng
   We at his feet may fall;
   We'll join the everlasting song,
   And crown him Lord of all.

161. Blest be the tie.

1 BLEST be the tie that binds
   Our hearts in Christian love;
   The fellowship of kindred minds
   Is like to that above.

2 Before our Father's throne
   We pour our ardent prayers;
   Our fears, our hopes, our aims are one,
   Our comforts and our cares.

3 We share our mutual woes,
   Our mutual burdens bear;
   And often for each other flows
   The sympathising tear.

4 When we asunder part,
   It gives us inward pain;
   But we shall still be joined in heart,
   And hope to meet again.

162. How Gentle. *Same tune.*

1 How gentle God's commands!
   How kind his precepts are!
   Come, cast your burdens on the Lord,
   And trust his constant care.

2 Beneath his watchful eye
   His saints securely dwell;
   That hand which bears all nature up
   Shall guard his children well.

3 Why should this anxious load
   Press down your weary mind?
   Haste to your heavenly Father's throne,
   And sweet refreshment find.

4 His goodness stands approved,
   Unchanged from day to day;
   I'll drop my burden at his feet,
   And bear a song away.

FAMILIAR HYMNS.

164. What a Friend.

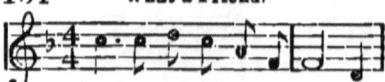

1. WHAT a Friend we have in Jesus,
   All our sins and griefs to bear!
   What a priveledge to carry
   Everything to God in prayer!
   O what peace we often forfeit,
   O what needless pain we bear,
   All because we do not carry
   Everything to God in prayer!

2. Have we trials and temptations?
   Is there trouble anywhere?
   We should never be discouraged,
   Take it to the Lord in prayer.
   Can we find a friend so faithful
   Who will all our sorrows share?
   Jesus knows our every weakness,
   Take it to the Lord in prayer.

165. Rock of Ages.

1. ROCK of Ages, cleft for me,
   Let me hide myself in thee;
   Let the water and the blood,
   From thy wounded side which flowed,
   Be of sin the double cure,
   Save from wrath and make me pure.

2. Could my tears forever flow,
   Could my zeal no languor know;
   These for sin could not atone;
   Thou must save, and thou alone;
   In my hand no price I bring,
   Simply to thy cross I cling.

3. While I draw this fleeting breath,
   When my eyes shall close in death,
   When I rise to worlds unknown,
   And behold thee on thy throne,
   Rock of Ages, cleft for me,
   Let me hide myself in thee.

166. Before the Cross.

1. MY faith looks up to thee,
   Thou Lamb of Calvary,
      Saviour divine;
   Now hear me while I pray,
   Take all my guilt away,
   O let me from this day
      Be wholly thine.

2. May thy rich grace impart
   Strength to my fainting heart,
      My zeal inspire;
   As thou hast died for me,
   O may my love to thee
   Pure, warm, and changeless be,—
      A living fire.

3. While life's dark maze I tread,
   And griefs around me spread,
      Be thou my guide;
   Bid darkness turn to day,
   Wipe sorrow's tears away,
   Nor let me ever stray
      From thee aside.

167. Happy Day.

1. O HAPPY day, that fixed my choice
   On thee, my Saviour and my God!
   Well may this glowing heart rejoice,
   And tell its rapture all abroad.

Cho.—Happy day, happy day,
   When Jesus washed my sins away;
   He taught me how to watch and pray,
   And live rejoicing every day;
   Happy day, happy day,
   When Jesus washed my sins away.

2. 'Tis done, the great transaction's done—
   I am my Lord's and he is mine;
   He drew me, and I followed on,
   Charmed to confess the voice divine.

3. Now rest, my long divided heart:
   Fixed on this blissful centre, rest
   Nor ever from thy Lord depart,
   With him of every good possessed.

168. Sweet Hour of Prayer.

1. Sweet hour of prayer, sweet hour of prayer,
   That calls me from a world of care,
   And bids me at my Father's throne
   Make all my wants and wishes known!
   In seasons of distress and grief
   My soul has often found relief,
   And oft escaped the tempter's snare
   By thy return, sweet hour of prayer.

2. Sweet hour of prayer, sweet hour of prayer,
   Thy wings shall my petition bear
   To him, whose truth and faithfulness
   Engage the waiting soul to bless;
   And since he bids me seek his face,
   Believe his word, and trust his grace,
   I'll cast on him my every care,
   And wait for thee, sweet hour of prayer.

Help Just a Little.

Music from "The Wells of Salvation," new words by Rev. W. A. Spencer.

Wm. J. Kirkpatrick.

1. Brother for Christ's kingdom sighing, Help a lit-tle, help a lit-tle;
2. Is thy cup made sad by tri-al? Help a lit-tle, help a lit-tle;
3. Though no wealth to thee is giv-en, Help a lit-tle, help a lit-tle;

Help to save the mil-lions dy-ing, Help just a lit-tle.
Sweet-en it with self-de-ni-al, Help just a lit-tle.
Sac-ri-fice is gold in heav-en, Help just a lit-tle.

CHORUS.
Oh, the wrongs that we may righten! Oh, the hearts that we may lighten!
Oh, the skies that we may brighten! Helping just a lit-tle.

4 Let us live for one another,
 Help a little, help a little;
 Help to lift each fallen brother,
 Help just a little.

5 Tho' thy life is pressed with sorrow,
 Help a little, help a little;
 Bravely look t'ward God's to-morrow,
 Help just a little.

Copyright, 1885, by John J. Hood.

170   Depth of Mercy.

1 DEPTH of mercy! can there be
  Mercy still reserved for me?
  Can my God his wrath forbear?
  Me, the chief of sinners, spare?
Cho.—God is love! I know, I feel;
  Jesus lives, and loves me still·
  Jesus lives,
  He lives and loves me still.

2 I have long withstood his grace,
  Long provoked him to his face:
  Would not hearken to his calls;
  Grieved him by a thousand falls.

3 Now incline me to repent;
  Let me now my sins lament;
  Now my foul revolt deplore,
  Weep, believe, and sin no more.

171   I Hear Thy Welcome Voice.

1 I HEAR thy welcome voice,
  That calls me, Lord, to thee,
  For cleansing in thy precious blood
  That flowed on Calvary.
Cho.—I am coming, Lord,
  Coming now to thee!
  Wash me, cleanse me in the blood
  That flowed on Calvary.

2 Though coming weak and vile,
  Thou dost my strength assure;
  Thou dost my vileness fully cleanse,
  Till spotless all and pure.

3 'Tis Jesus calls me on
  To perfect faith and love,
  To perfect hope, and peace, and trust,
  For earth and heaven above.

4 All hail, atoning blood!
  All hail, redeeming grace!
  All hail, the gift of Christ our Lord,
  Our Strength and Righteousness!

172   The Home Over There.

1 OH, think of the home over there,
  By the side of the river of light,
  Where the saints, all immortal and fair,
  Are robed in their garments of white.
Ref.—Over there, over there,
  Oh, think of the home over there.

2 Oh, think of the friends over there,
  Who before us the journey have trod,
  Of the songs that they breathe on the air,
  In their home in the palace of God.

Ref.—Over there, over there,
  Oh, think of the friends over there.

3 My Saviour is now over there,
  There my kindred and friends are at rest;
  Then away from my sorrow and care,
  Let me fly to the land of the blest.
Ref.—Over there, over there,
  My Saviour is now over there.

4 I'll soon be at home over there,
  For the end of my journey I see;
  Many dear to my heart, over there,
  Are watching and waiting for me.
Ref.—Over there, over there,
  I'll soon be at home over there.

173   He Leadeth Me!

1 HE leadeth me! O blessed thought!
  O words with heavenly comfort fraught!
  Whate'er I do, where'er I be,
  Still 'tis God's hand that leadeth me.
Cho.—He leadeth me, he leadeth me,
  By his own hand he leadeth me:
  His faithful follower I would be,
  For by his hand he leadeth me.

2 Sometimes 'mid scenes of deepest gloom,
  Sometimes where Eden's bowers bloom,
  By waters still, o'er troubled sea,—
  Still 'tis his hand that leadeth me!

3 Lord, I would clasp thy hand in mine,
  Nor ever murmur nor repine,
  Content, whatever lot I see,
  Since 'tis my God that leadeth me!

174   My Country! 'tis of Thee.

1 MY country! 'tis of thee,
  Sweet land of liberty,
    Of thee I sing:
  Land where my fathers died!
  Land of the pilgrims' pride!
  From every mountain side
    Let freedom ring!

2 My native country, thee,
  Land of the noble, free,
    Thy name I love;
  I love thy rocks and rills,
  Thy woods and templed hills:
  My heart with rapture thrills
    Like that above.

3 Our fathers' God! to thee,
  Author of liberty,
    To thee we sing;
  Long may our land be bright
  With freedom's holy light;
  Protect us by thy might,
    Great God, our King!

FAMILIAR HYMNS.

176. Saviour, like a Shepherd.

1 SAVIOUR, like a shepherd lead us,
   Much we need thy tend'rest care,
   In thy pleasant pastures feed us,
   For our use thy folds prepare;
   ||: Blessed Jesus, blessed Jesus,
   Thou hast bought us, thine we are. :||

2 We are thine, do thou befriend us,
   Be the Guardian of our way;
   Keep thy flock, from sin defend us,
   Seek us when we go astray;
   ||: Blessed Jesus, blessed Jesus,
   Hear, oh, hear us when we pray. :||

3 Thou hast promised to receive us,
   Poor and sinful though we be;
   Thou hast mercy to relieve us,
   Grace to cleanse, and power to free;
   ||: Blessed Jesus, blessed Jesus,
   We will early turn to thee. :||

177. I Love to Tell the Story.

1 I LOVE to tell the Story
   Of unseen things above,
   Of Jesus and his glory,
   Of Jesus and his love;
   I love to tell the Story,
   Because I know it's true;
   It satisfies my longings,
   As nothing else would do.

   Cho.—I love to tell the Story!
      'Twill be my theme in glory,
      To tell the Old, Old Story
      Of Jesus and his love.

2 I love to tell the Story!
   More wonderful it seems,
   Than all the golden fancies
   Of all our golden dreams;
   I love to tell the Story!
   It did so much for me;
   And that is just the reason
   I tell it now to thee.

3 I love to tell the Story!
   For those who know it best
   Seem hungering and thirsting
   To hear it, like the rest;
   And when, in scenes of glory,
   I sing the NEW, NEW SONG,
   'Twill be the OLD, OLD STORY
   That I have loved so long.

178. Jesus, Lover of My Soul.

1 JESUS, lover of my soul,
   Let me to thy bosom fly,
   While the nearer waters roll,
   While the tempest still is high.
   Hide me, O my Saviour, hide,
   Till the storm of life is past;
   Safe into the haven guide,
   O, receive my soul at last.

2 Other refuge have I none;
   Hangs my helpless soul on thee:
   Leave, oh, leave me not alone,
   Still support and comfort me:
   All my trust on thee is stayed,
   All my help from thee I bring;
   Cover my defenceless head
   With the shadow of thy wing!

3 Thou, O Christ, art all I want;
   More than all in thee I find;
   Raise the fallen, cheer the faint,
   Heal the sick, and lead the blind.
   Just and holy is thy name,
   I am all unrighteousness:
   False and full of sin I am,
   Thou art full of truth and grace.

4 Plenteous grace with thee is found,
   Grace to cover all my sin;
   Let the healing streams abound;
   Make and keep me pure within.
   Thou of life the fountain art,
   Freely let me take of thee:
   Spring thou up within my heart,
   Rise to all eternity.

179. There is a Land.

1 THERE is a land of pure delight,
   Where saints immortal reign;
   Eternal day excludes the night,
   And pleasures banish pain;
   There everlasting Spring abides,
   And never-whith'ring flowers;
   Death, like a narrow sea, divides
   This heavenly land from ours.

2 Sweet fields beyond the swelling flood
   Stand dressed in living green;
   So to the Jews old Canaan stood,
   While Jordan rolled between;
   Could we but climb where Moses stood,
   And view the landscape o'er, [flood
   Not Jordan's stream, nor death's cold
   Should fright us from the shore.

181 More Faith in Jesus.

HENRIETTA E. BLAIR.   WM. J. KIRKPATRICK.

1. While struggling thro' this vale of tears I want more faith in Je-sus; A-
2. To war against the foes with-in I want more faith in Je-sus; To
3. To brave the storms that here I meet I want more faith in Je-sus; To
4. I want a faith that works by love, A constant faith in Je-sus; A

mid tempta-tions, cares, and fears, I want more faith in Je-sus.
rise a-bove the powers of sin I want more faith in Je-sus.
rest con-fid-ing at his feet I want more faith in Je-sus.
faith that mountains can remove, A liv-ing faith in Je-sus.

D. S.—And this my cry, as time rolls by, I want more faith in Je-sus.

want more faith, I want more faith, A clearer, brighter, stronger faith in Jesus;

Copyright, 1885, by JOHN J. HOOD.

182   Beulah Land.

1 I'VE reached the land of corn and wine,
And all its riches freely mine;
Here shines undimmed one blissful day,
For all my night has passed away.

CHO.—O Beulah land, sweet Beulah land,
As on thy highest mount I stand,
I look away across the sea,
Where mansions are prepared for me,
And view the shining glory shore,
My heaven, my home, for evermore!

2 My Saviour comes and walks with me,
And sweet communion here have we,
He gently leads me by his hand,
For this is heaven's border-land.

3 A sweet perfume upon the breeze
Is borne from ever-vernal trees,
And flowers that never-fading grow
Where streams of life forever flow.

4 The zephyrs seem to float to me
Sweet sounds of heaven's melody,
As angels with the white-robed throng
Join in the sweet redemption song.

MELODIOUS SONNETS

FOR

SACRED SERVICE

BY

JOHN R. SWENEY AND WM. J. KIRKPATRICK.

"*Teach me some Melodious Sonnet.*"

PHILADELPHIA: JOHN J. HOOD, 1018 ARCH ST.

COPYRIGHT, 1885, BY JOHN J. HOOD.

COPYRIGHT, 1885, BY JOHN J. HOOD.

*"Teach me some Melodious Sonnet,
Sung by flaming tongues above."*

———◇———

IN response to the call made by the foregoing lines we have endeavored to supply the "Melodious Sonnets." We do so knowing that it is alone the Holy Spirit can attune the heart of man to the music of the heavenly choir; but we trust our sonnets may be found suitable channels for the higher and holier melodies.

THE COMPILERS.

MELODIOUS SONNETS may be had with music in character notation or in the ordinary notation. Please mention style preferred when ordering.

No person may PRINT, for sale or otherwise, any copyright hymn of this collection without permission being duly obtained in writing.

183. Jesus is Good to Me.

Rev. E. H. Stokes, D. D.
Jno. R. Sweney.

1. I love my Saviour, his heart is good, He has loved me o'er and o'er;
2. He calls, I rise, and he maketh me whole,—How fond his tender embrace!
3. I want to love him with all my heart, Tho' all its powers are small;
4. He's good to me in my sorrow's night, He's good in the tempest's roll;

He sought me wand'ring, I'm saved by his blood, And I love him more and more.
He cleanses and keeps me and blesses my soul'—My day the smile of his face.
I will not keep from him any part, For he is worthy of all.
He bringeth from darkness into light,—With joy he filleth my soul.

CHORUS.

Je-sus is good to me, . . . Je-sus is good to me; . . .
    to me,   to me;
So good! so good! Je-sus is good to my soul.

Copyright, 1885, by John J. Hood.   Temple Trio—L

185 **Wonderful Love of Jesus.**

"The love of Christ, which passeth knowledge."
Eph iii. 19.

E. D. Mund.   E. S. Lorenz.

1. In vain in high and ho-ly lays My soul her grateful voice would raise; For
2. A joy by day, a peace by night, In storms a calm, in darkness light; In
3. My hope for pardon when I call, My trust for lift-ing when I fall; In

who can sing the worthy praise Of the won-derful love of Je-sus?
pain a balm, in weakness might, Is the won-derful love of Je-sus.
life, in death, my all in all, Is the won-derful love of Je-sus.

CHORUS.

Won-derful love! won-derful love! Won-der-ful love of Je-sus!

Wonder-ful love! won-derful love! Wonder-ful love of Je-sus!

From "Holy Voices," by per.

The Beautiful Hills.—CONCLUDED.

rap - turous sight Of the beau - tiful glory-crowned hills. beautiful hills.

187. Jesus our Redeemer.

FRANK GOULD.
JNO. R. SWENEY.

1. Jus-ti-fied by faith in thee, Peace with God henceforth have we;
2. Thou thyself our debt hast paid, Full a-tonement thou hast made;
3. Once condemned but now reprieved, In-to life through grace received;
4. While from grace to grace we go, More and more thy love bestow,

From the law we now are free, Je-sus our blessed Redeem-er.
On thy head our guilt was laid, Je-sus our blessed Redeem-er.
Oh, what joy since we believed, Je-sus our blessed Redeem-er.
Till thy per-fect bliss we know, Je-sus our blessed Redeem-er.

D.S.—From the law we now are free, Je-sus our blessed Redeem-er.

CHORUS. D.S.

Not un-to us, not un-to us, On-ly thine the praise shall be.

Copyright, 1884, by JOHN J. HOOD.

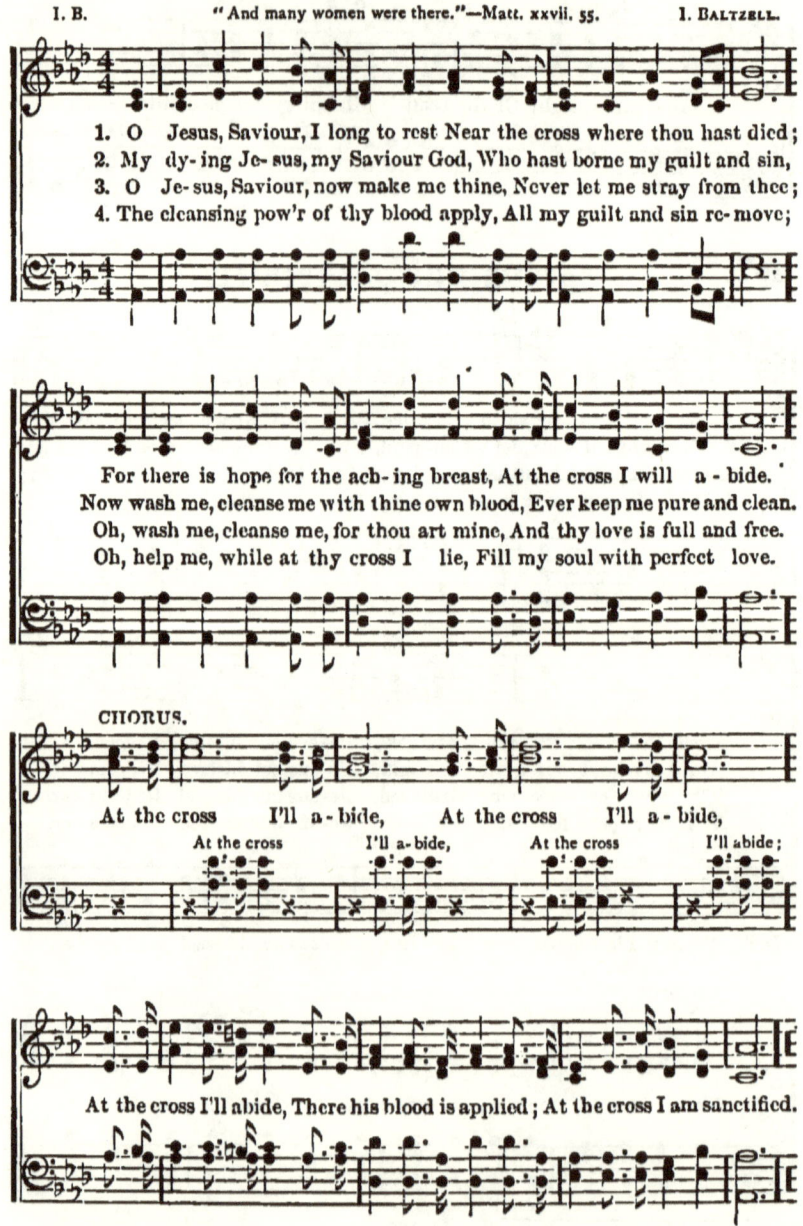

191. The Waiting Guest.

Mrs. R. N. Turner.   Wm. J. Kirkpatrick.

1. Who is this that waiteth, Waiteth for my call, While the dews of morning
2. Who is this that waiteth In the storm outside, Sad and worn and weary,
3. O, it is my Saviour! Saw I not be-fore All that bleeding sorrow,
4. Thou shalt wait no longer In the gloom outside! Enter, O sweet Stranger,

Gently round him fall? Hark! I hear him knocking, Knocking at my door,
Still his wish de-nied? O, such gentle patience Must an entrance win;
All that anguish sore? Saw I not the nail-prints, When his blood was shed?
And with me a-bide! Long I sought thee, Saviour, Thou wast at my door!

CHORUS.

Asking me for entrance,—Pleading o'er and o'er! ⎫
Still I hear him pleading, "Let me enter in." ⎬ Let me in, let me in,
Saw I not the thorn-crown On his king-ly head? ⎪
Now I bid thee welcome, Welcome ev-er-more! ⎭ O come in, O come in,

Patiently I wait? Wilt thou not unbar the door Ere it be too late?
Be my guest to-day; Saviour, come, abide with me Ev-ermore, I pray.

Copyright, 1884, by John J Hood.

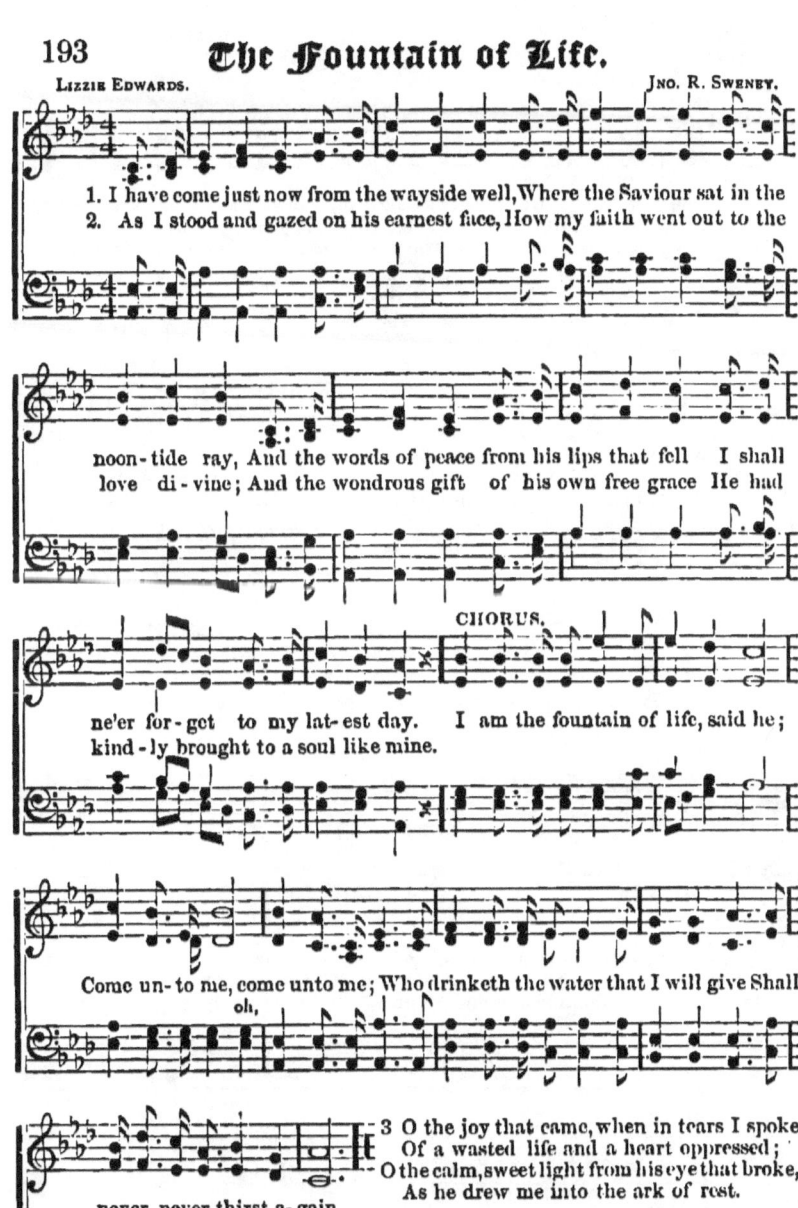

Will You Go?—CONCLUDED.

saints are clothed in white? Go where the saved shall find no night, But endless day?

195 Rouse, Ye Saints.

C. H. YATMAN.
W. H. GEISTWEIT.

With spirit.

1. Rouse, ye saints, the world is dy-ing, We must work while it is day;
2. Wake, ye men, let us be do-ing, While the sun is in the sky;
3. Je-sus, Saviour, help our spir-its, That we nev-er wea-ry be

Sin-ners lost to us are cry-ing For the strait and narrow way.
Let us seek the weak and er-ring, Precious souls that soon may die.
Lead-ing sin-ners to the Fountain Ev-er flowing, full and free.

CHORUS.

We will work from morn till night, By the Spir-it's power and might

Lead-ing men un-to the Light, Bles-sed Light of Day!

Copyright, 1885, by JOHN J. HOOD.

196. Witnessing Spirit.

Rev. Jno. O. Foster, A. M.
Jno. R. Sweney.

1. O come, Holy Spirit, and help us to sing The praises eternal of Jesus our King; Our hope is in thee, and on thee we rely; Without thee we suffer, and languish, and die.
2. From Deity's bosom descend, gentle dove. We ask for thy fulness, we covet thy love; We grope in the darkness, if trusting our might, We shout in our gladness, when walking in light.
3. Now waiting, believing, we have the glad sign,— Thy whispering presence is knowledge divine; Perfumed by thy breathings we're loaded with balm, And Eden is gained thro' the blood of the Lamb.
4. O Spirit eternal, forever abide, Our Leader, Defender, Protector, and Guide; Through all of life's journey, whatever is given, Direct us in safety to mansions in heav[en]

CHORUS.

Spirit most holy,

Copyright, 1884, by John J. Hood.

Witnessing Spirit.—CONCLUDED.

Light of my heart, Joy of the low-ly, Glo-ry impart!
Light of my heart, of my heart, Joy of the low-ly, the low-ly, Glory, oh, glory impart!

197 Flow In.

"He that hath the Son hath life."—1 John v. 12.

Miss Abbie Mills.   Wm. J. Kirkpatrick.

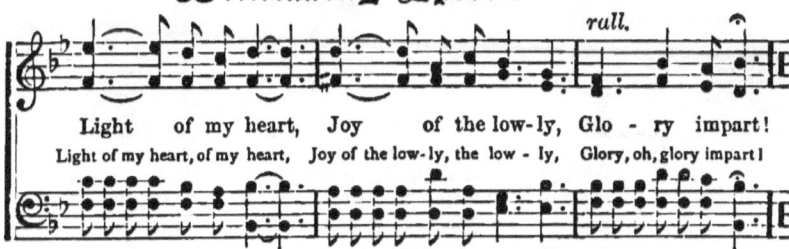

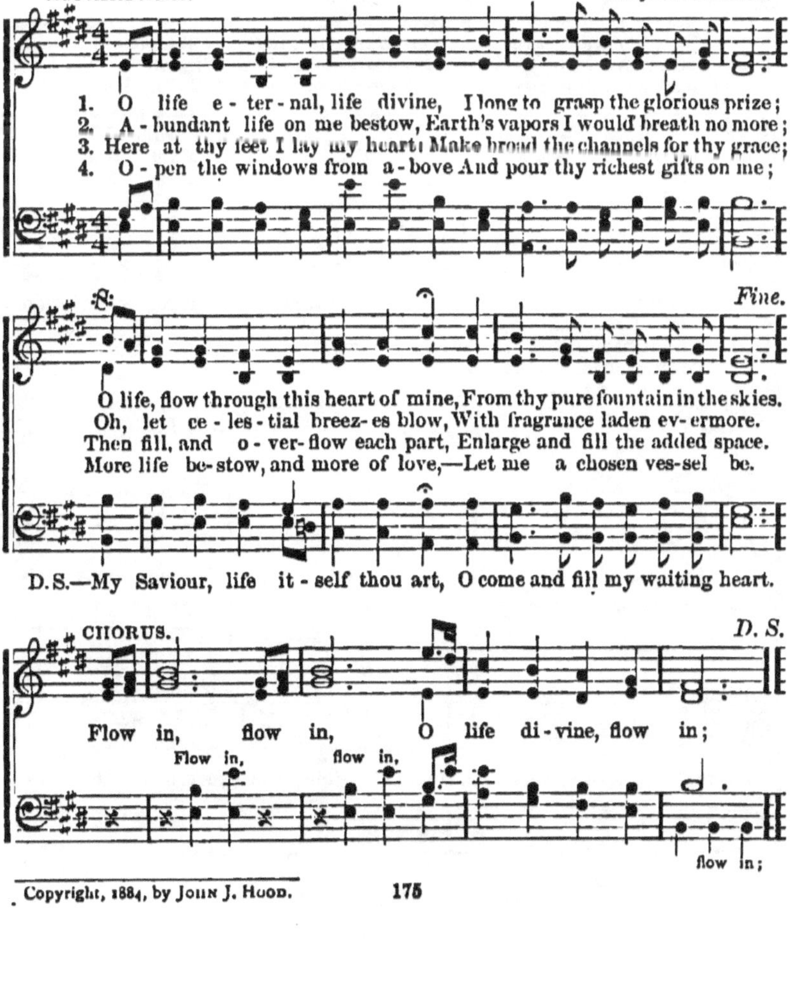

1. O life e-ter-nal, life divine, I long to grasp the glorious prize;
2. A-bundant life on me bestow, Earth's vapors I would breath no more;
3. Here at thy feet I lay my heart; Make broad the channels for thy grace;
4. O-pen the windows from a-bove And pour thy richest gifts on me;

O life, flow through this heart of mine, From thy pure fountain in the skies.
Oh, let ce-les-tial breez-es blow, With fragrance laden ev-ermore.
Then fill, and o-ver-flow each part, Enlarge and fill the added space.
More life be-stow, and more of love,—Let me a chosen ves-sel be.

D.S.—My Saviour, life it-self thou art, O come and fill my waiting heart.

CHORUS.   D. S.

Flow in,   flow in,   O life di-vine, flow in;
  Flow in,   flow in,
                                              flow in;

Copyright, 1884, by John J. Hood.

198. Onward Now!

Mrs. Van Alstyne.
Thro. F. Seward. By per.

1. On-ward now! the trum-pet call is sounding: On-ward now! with
2. On-ward now! be valiant, brave and dar-ing; On-ward now, the
3. On-ward now! our King has gone be-fore us; Strong in him, our
4. On-ward now! be firm and faithful ev - er; On-ward now, our

ho-ly rapture bounding, Heart and voice in har-mo-ny resound-ing,
Christian armor wear-ing; On-ward now! the roy-al standard bearing,
triumph will be glorious. On-ward now! his lov-ing care is o'er us;
cour-age failing nev-er, Look-ing home, beyond the si-lent riv-er—

REFRAIN.

Sweetly join the chorus of the skies. Praise our God, who reigneth evermore;
Let our songs in happy concert rise.
In his hand behold the heav'nly prize.
Looking home, where pleasure never dies.

Praise our God: his bless-ed name a-dore. On-ward now! his

might-y love proclaiming, Sweet-ly join the cho-rus of the skies.

Copyright, 1883, by T. F. Seward.

199. Eden Shore.

Mrs. M. A. Kidder. — W. H. Doane.

1. On the sweet Eden shore, so peaceful and bright, The spirits made perfect are dwelling in light; Their white wings are wafting them gently along, Through beautiful regions of glory and song.
2. O blessed to rise when life's pangs are o'er, To mount up to heaven and dwell ev-ermore, To nev-er grow weary, and nev-er know care, In those beautiful regions, so blooming and fair.
3. On the sweet Eden shore, the home of the blest, With friends gone before soon we'll tarry and rest; Content there with Jesus our Saviour to stay, We'll delight in the pleasures that never decay.

CHORUS.

On the sweet Eden shore, so peaceful and bright; On the sweet Eden shore, the home of the blest, With friends gone before we'll tarry and rest, Tarry and rest, tarry and rest on the shore.

By permission.

Temple Trio—M

203. The Future.

Miss JENNIE STOUT. A. A. ARMEN.

1. Oh, I oft-en sit and pon-der, When the sun is sink-ing low,
2. Shall I be at work for Je-sus, Whilst he leads me by the hand,
3. But perhaps my work for Je-sus Soon in fu-ture may be done,

Where shall yonder fu-ture find me: Does but God in heav-en know?
And to those a-round be say-ing, Come and join his hap-py band?
All my earthly tri-als end-ed, And my crown in heav-en won;

Shall I be a-mong the liv-ing? Shall I min-gle with the free?
Come, for all things now are rea-dy, Come, his faithful foll-'wer be;
Then for-ev-er with the ran-somed Thro' e-ter-ni-ty I'd be

Where-so-e'er my path be lead-ing, Saviour, keep my heart with thee.
Oh, where'er my path be lead-ing, Saviour, keep my heart with thee.
Chanting hymns to him who bought me With his blood shed on the tree.

CHORUS.

Oh, the fu — — — ture lies be-fore me, And I
Oh, the fu-ture lies be-fore me, And I know not where I'll be, Oh, the

From "Our Sabbath Home," by per.

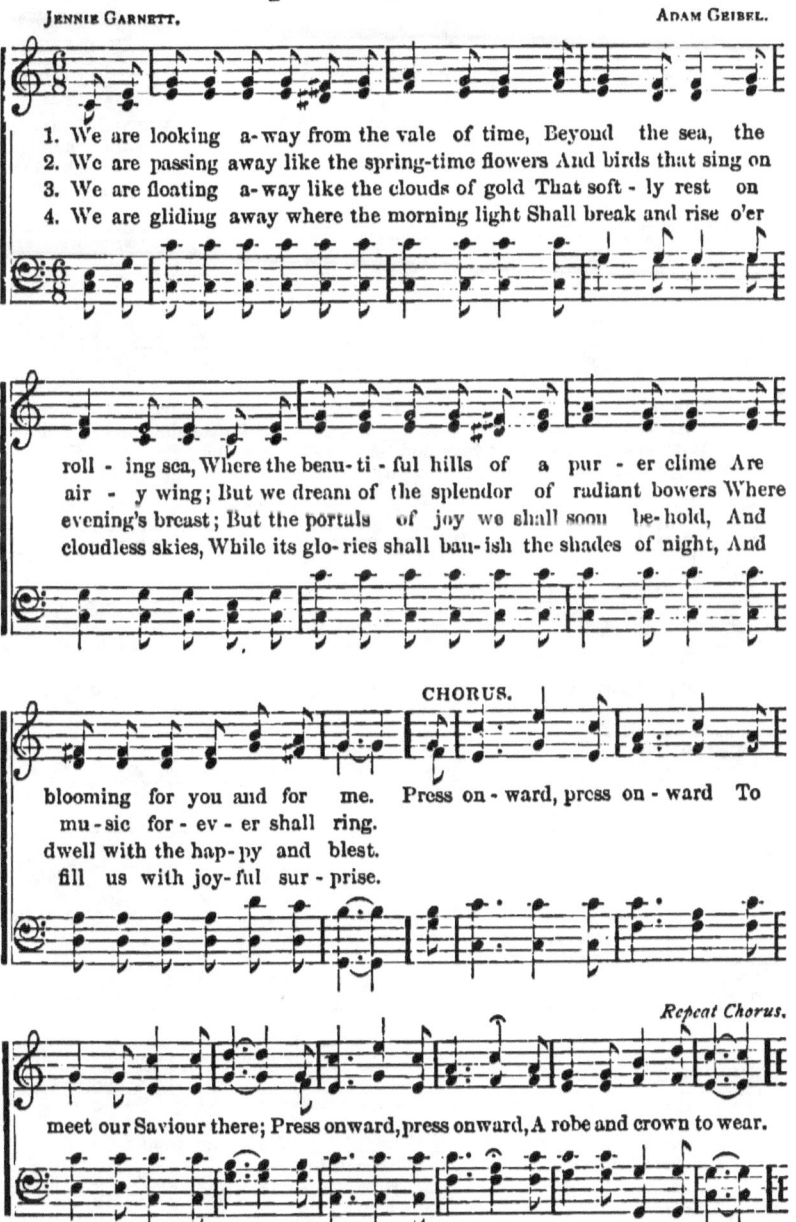

212. My Hope and my Glory.

FANNY J. CROSBY.   CHAS. EDW. PRIOR.

1. I am walking with the Lord, and be-lieving in his word, I am
2. Now my way is growing bright, and my soul is full of light, My Re-
3. I was once a burdened soul, but my Saviour made me whole, his re-

hap-py as a heart can be; I am sing-ing all the day how he
deemer's guiding hand I see; If a thousand worlds were mine, I would
demption all my theme shall be; I will sing it till I die, and pro-

D. S.—I am sing-ing all the day how he

Fine. CHORUS.

washed my sins away Thro' the precious blood he shed for me. O the
glad-ly all resign For the rapture of his love to me.
claim beyond the sky What the grace of God has done for me.

washed my sins away Thro' the precious blood he shed for me.

D. S.

cross where my Saviour hath bless'd me My hope and my glo-ry shall be;

Copyright, 1884, by JOHN J. HOOD.

213. A Song of Trust.

"For the Lord thy God bringeth thee into a good land, a land of brooks of water, of fountains, and depths that spring out of valleys and hills." "And I will give her the valley of Achor for a door of hope: and she shall sing there."

"BEULAH." GRACE WEISER.

1. God has given me a song, a song of trust, song of trust, And I sing it all day long, for sing I must; sing I must; Ev-'ry hour it sweeter grows, Fills my soul with blest re-pose, Just how rest-ful no one knows but those who trust.

2. O, I sing it on the mountain, in the light, Where the radiance of God's sunshine makes all bright; All my path seems bright and clear, Heav'nly land seems very near; Why, I almost then appear to walk by sight.

3. And I sing it in the valley dark and low, When my heart is crush'd with sor-row, pain, and woe; Then the shadows flee a-way, Like the night when dawns the day; Trust in God brings light alway, I find it so.

4. When I sing it in the desert parched and dry, Living streams begin to flow, a rich supply; Verdure in abundance grows, Deserts blossom like a rose, And my heart with joy o'erflows at God's reply.

5. For I've crossed the river Jordan, and I stand In the blessed land of promise,—Beulah land: Trusting is like breathing here, Just as easy,—doubt and fear Van-ish in this at-mosphere, in Beu-lah land.

CHORUS.

Ye who trust in the Lord, Oh, sing a glad refrain; Raise your songs on

Copyright, 1885, by JOHN J. HOOD.   192   From "Melodious Sonnets," by per.

A Song of Trust.—CONCLUDED.

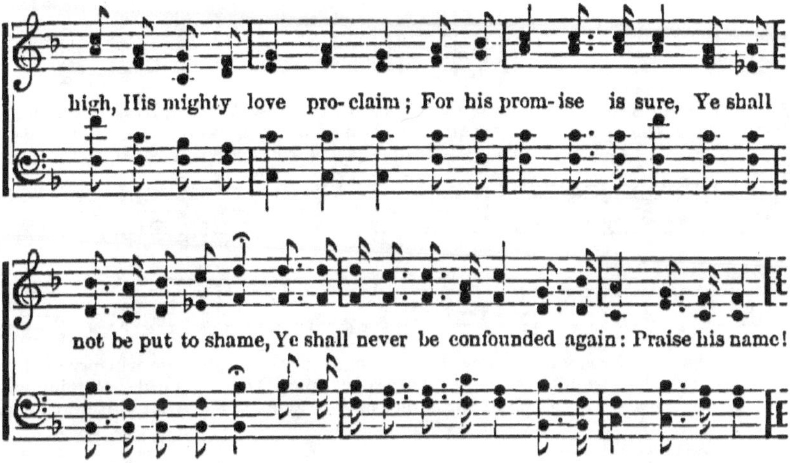

high, His mighty love pro-claim; For his prom-ise is sure, Ye shall not be put to shame, Ye shall never be confounded again: Praise his name!

214 Surrendered.

H. L. G.
Dr. H. L. Gilmour.

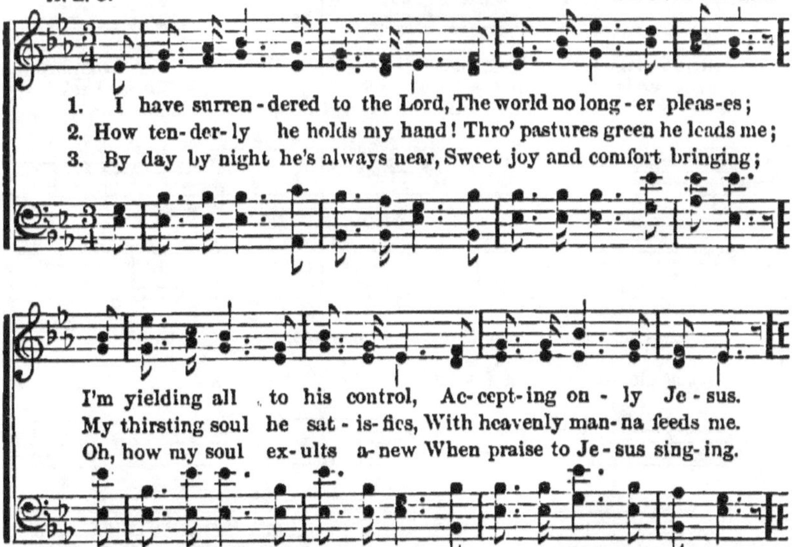

1. I have surren-dered to the Lord, The world no long-er pleas-es;
2. How ten-der-ly he holds my hand! Thro' pastures green he leads me;
3. By day by night he's always near, Sweet joy and comfort bringing;

I'm yielding all to his control, Ac-cept-ing on-ly Je-sus.
My thirsting soul he sat-is-fies, With heavenly man-na feeds me.
Oh, how my soul ex-ults a-new When praise to Je-sus sing-ing.

4 No noonday drought affects my soul,
In Jesus I'm confiding;
Oh, constant, sweet companionship,
With Christ in me abiding.

5 Oh, victory that's always sure!
Oh, blest emancipation!
Oh, vanquished tempter of my soul!
Oh, free and full salvation!

Copyright, 1885, by John J. Hood.

From "Melodious Sonnets," by per.

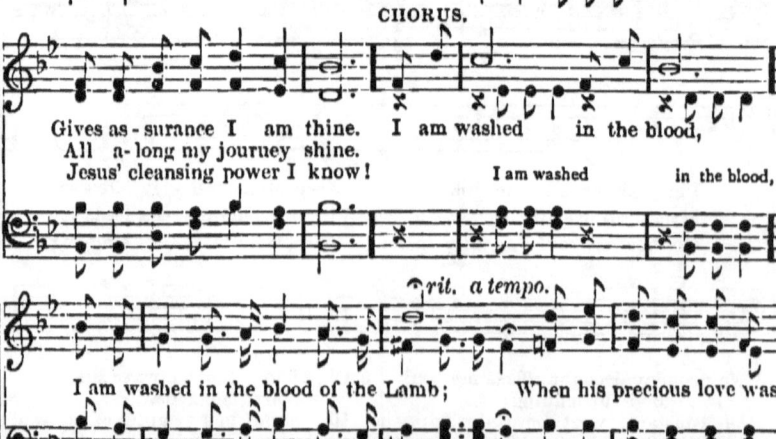

217

PRISCILLA J. OWENS. WM. J. KIRKPATRICK.

1. Our heav'nly habi - tation Above the tempest stands, Where breezes of sal-
va - tion Flow o'er Immanuel's lands; And there, when toil is done, And
peace with vict'ry won, The dawn shall meet life's setting sun, At home, at

2. Tho' here the storms are swelling And floods of sorrow foam, We know we have a
dwell-ing, A sure a-bid-ing home; The Saviour's loving breast Was
pierced to make that rest; O seek this ref-uge, ye distressed, And be at

D. S.—joy and peace for - ev - ermore, At home, at

Fine. CHORUS. *D. S.*

home with Je-sus. At home with Je-sus, At home with Jesus, There's

3 His arms of strength shall hold thee
  Above the tempter's snare,
  His shadow sweet enfold thee
  Amid the furnace glare.
  Pass joyful on thy way,
  And in each trial say,
  "His presence is my hope and stay,
  At home, at home with Jesus."

4 Across death's rolling river
  True friends have gone before;
  We miss them here forever,
  We'll find them on life's shore.
  And glad each voice shall blend,
  When friend shall welcome friend,
  And ceaseless songs of praise ascend,
  At home, at home with Jesus.

Copyright, 1884, by JOHN J. HOOD.

221. In the King's Highway.

Fanny J. Crosby.   Jno. R. Sweney.

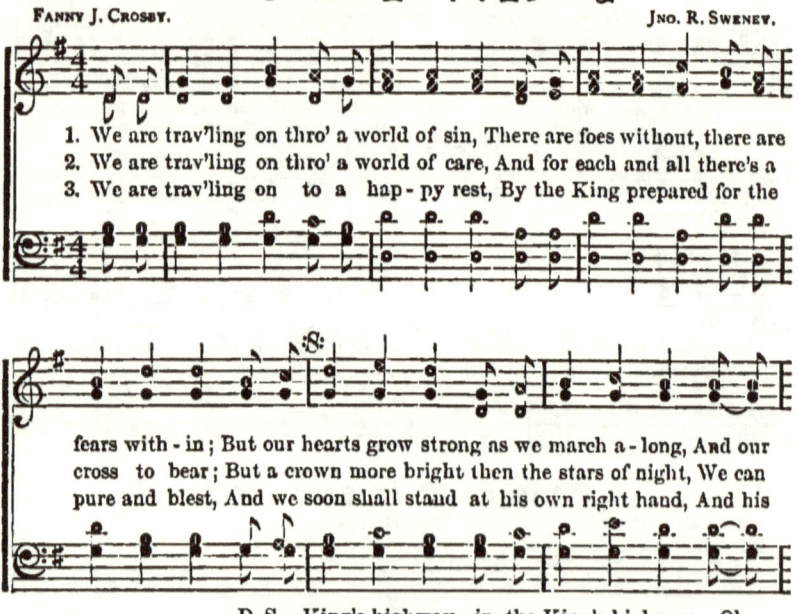

1. We are trav'ling on thro' a world of sin, There are foes without, there are fears with-in; But our hearts grow strong as we march a-long, And our steps keep time to the joy-ful song. We are going, going home to the
2. We are trav'ling on thro' a world of care, And for each and all there's a cross to bear; But a crown more bright then the stars of night, We can see by faith at the gates of life.
3. We are trav'ling on to a hap-py rest, By the King prepared for the pure and blest, And we soon shall stand at his own right hand, And his wel-come hear in the soul's fair land.

D. S.—King's highway, in the King's highway, Oh, glo-ry be to God! in the King's highway.

Fine. CHORUS.

realms of day, We are going, going home in the King's highway; In the

Copyright, 1884, by John J. Hood.

223. Strive to Enter in.

HENRIETTA E. BLAIR.
WM. J. KIRKPATRICK.

1. At the gate that leads to glory, from the rugged path of sin, Where the joys that fill the soul are ever new, O ye weary, heav-y-laden, will you strive to en-ter in, While the Saviour now is waiting there for you?
2. At the gate that leads to glory there's a light that shineth still, 'Tis the pure and holy light of promise true; Hear the blessed invi-tation to the who-so-ev-er will, From the Saviour who is waiting now for you.
3. At the gate that leads to glory you will never knock in vain, There is room for ev'ry one, and welcome, too; Only give your heart to Jesus, life e-ter-nal you will gain: He is call-ing, he is waiting now for you.
4. From the gate that leads to glory, oh, how man-y go astray! We are told that they that find it are but few; Then believe the words of Jesus, enter quickly while you may: He is waiting now with o-pen arms for you.

CHORUS.

Strait is the gate and narrow is the way That leadeth unto life a-bove;

Strive to en-ter in, oh, strive to en-ter in! Come to a Saviour's love!

Copyright, 1884, by JOHN J HOOD.

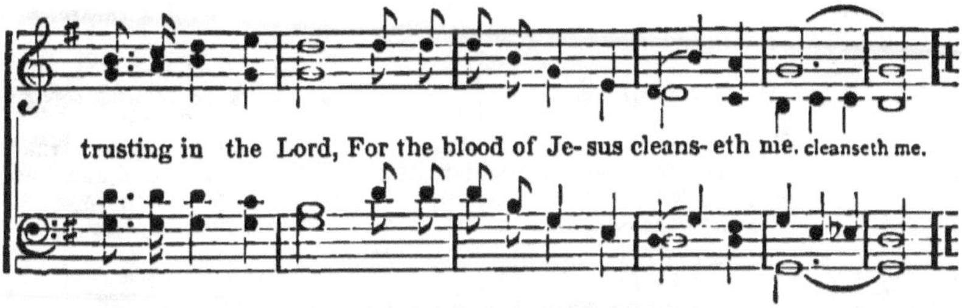

Believing and Receiving.—CONCLUDED.

trusting in the Lord, For the blood of Jesus cleanseth me. cleanseth me.

226. Calling You and Me.

S Martin. CHILDREN'S HYMN. Jno. R. Sweney.

1. 'Tis the Shepherd's voice we hear Calling you and me; To the precious fold so dear, Calling you and me.
2. He is ev-er watching nigh, Calling you and me; Looking down from yonder sky, Calling you and me.
3. Where the sweetest flowers grow, Calling you and me; Where the brightest waters flow, Calling you and me.
4. To his gen-tle, loving breast, Calling you and me; Where the lambs in safety rest, Calling you and me.

CHORUS.

Many times in ev'ry day We can hear him in our play, Calling to the better way, Calling you and me.

Copyright, 1885, by John J. Hood.

Follow Jesus.—CONCLUDED.

Follow Je-sus on to Zi - on: Je-sus is a faithful guide.
on to Zi-on, on to Zi-on,

---

232 ## Lean on Him.

FANNY J. CROSBY.   JNO R. SWENEY.

1. Troubled heart, thy fear dis-pel; He who loves and loves thee well,
2. Troubled heart, oh, why dismayed? Let thy hope on God be stayed;
3. Troubled heart, despond no more, He who once thy sor-row bore,
4. Troubled heart, be still, be still, Learn to know thy Saviour's will;

Though thy star of faith is dim, Kind-ly bids thee lean on him.
Go to him whose name is love; Prayer will ev-'ry cloud re-move.
He who wept on earth for thee, Ev-'ry tear of thine can see.
He thy dear-est friend will be, Lean on him who died for thee.

D. S.—What-so-e'er thy tri-al be, Lean on him who cares for thee.

CHORUS.   D. S.

Lean on him, lean on him, Though the light of faith is dim;

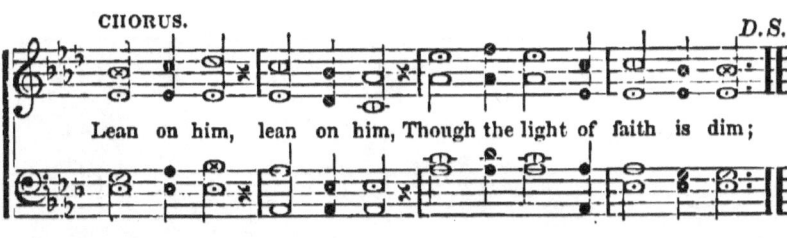

Copyright, 1884, by JOHN J. HOOD.

237. Until Ye Find.

Rev. E. H. Stokes, D. D.
Luke xv.
Jno. R. Sweney.

Andante con espress.

1. A-las! a-las! a wayward sheep Had wandered from the fold, Far o'er the mountains rough and steep, Where howling tempests rolled; The Shepherd, with a burdened mind, Went forth the missing one to find, The miss-ing one, far, far a-way, The miss-ing one to find.

2. He sought with many-a footstep sore, From early morn till night; Thro' rock-y wastes, where torrents roar,—All pathways but the right; Then cried, with sad and burdened mind, The missing I have failed to find, The miss-ing one, far, far a-way, A-las! I've failed to find.

3. How long, O Lord, must I still go? How long search for the sheep? They've wandered far a-way, I know,—Discouraged, lo, I weep: How long thus go, with burdened mind? "Go," Jesus saith, "until ye find;" The miss-ing one must not be lost,—Go, seek un-til ye find!

CHORUS.

Go, seek un-til ye find; Go, seek un-til ye find; The

Chorus to last verse:—
Joy! joy! the lost is found; Joy! joy! the lost is found; The

Copyright, 1885, by John J. Hood.

Until Ye Find.—CONCLUDED.

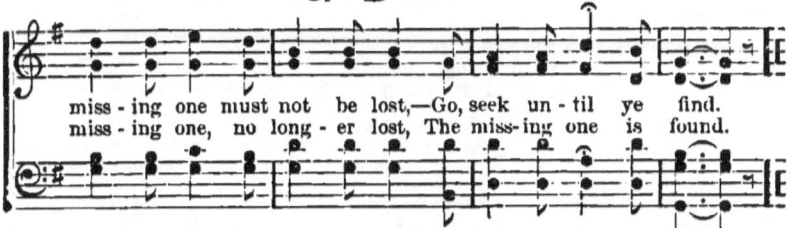

miss - ing one must not be lost,—Go, seek un - til ye find.
miss - ing one, no long - er lost, The miss-ing one is found.

4 I've sought my friends for many-a day,
Have prayed for many-a year;
Yet, still they wander far away,
O'er mountains dark and drear;
How long thus seek with burdened mind?
"Seek," Jesus saith, "until ye find;"
The missing one must not be lost,—
"Go, seek until ye find!"

5 Lord, at thy word I go again,
Believing I shall find;
I listened, and a low refrain
Came to me on the wind;
Led by the sadly joyful sound
I rushed, and, lo, the lost was found!
Joy! joy! O blessed joy divine!
The lost one I have found.

238 Trustingly.

H. BONAR.   WM. J. KIRKPATRICK.

1. Trust - ing - ly, trust - ing - ly, Je - sus, to thee Come I; Lord,
2. Peace - ful - ly, peace - ful - ly Walk I with thee; Je - sus, my
3. Hap - pi - ly, hap - pi - ly Pass I a - long, Ea - ger to

lov - ing - ly, Come thou to me! Then shall I lov - ing - ly,
Lord, thou art All, all to me; Peace thou hast left to us,
work for thee, Ear - nest and strong; Life is for ser - vice true,

rit.

Then shall I joy - ful - ly walk here with thee, Walk here with thee.
Thy peace hast giv-en us; So let it be, So let it be.
Life is for bat - tle, too, Life is for song, Life is for song.

Copyright, 1885, by JOHN J. HOOD.

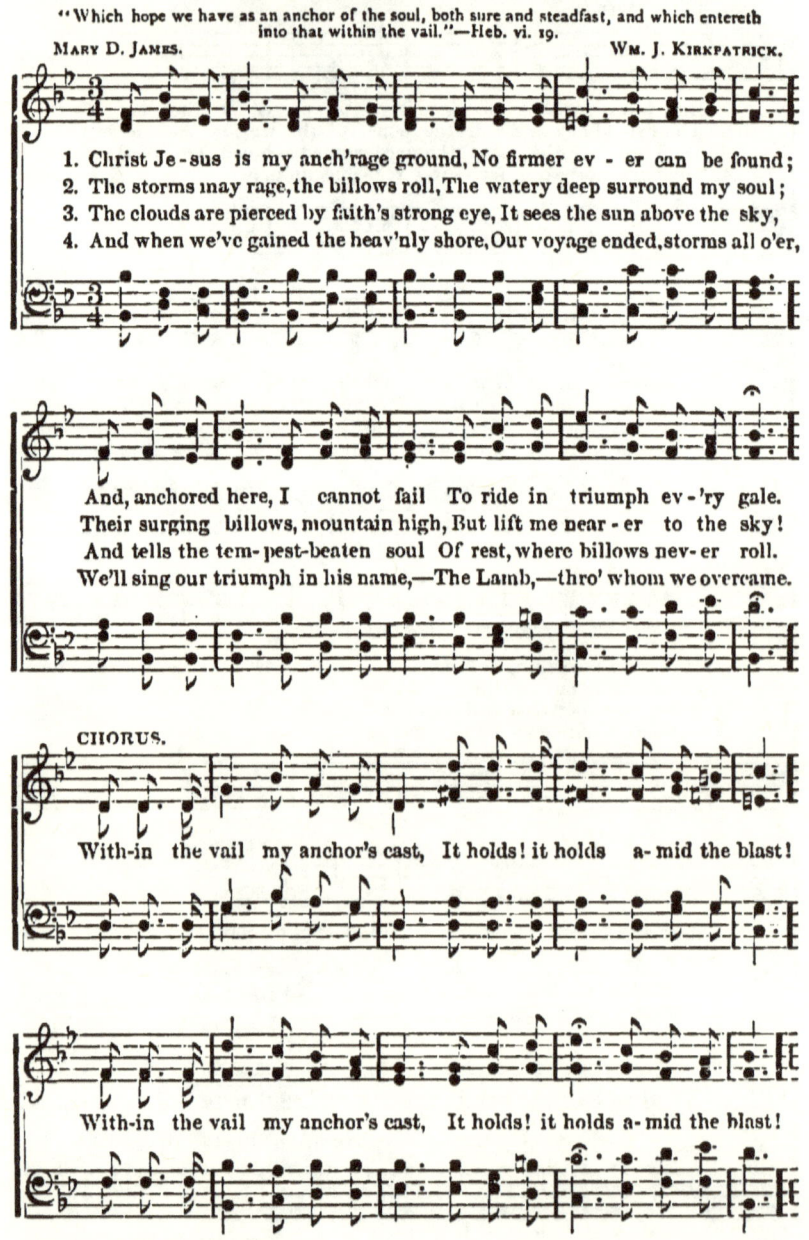

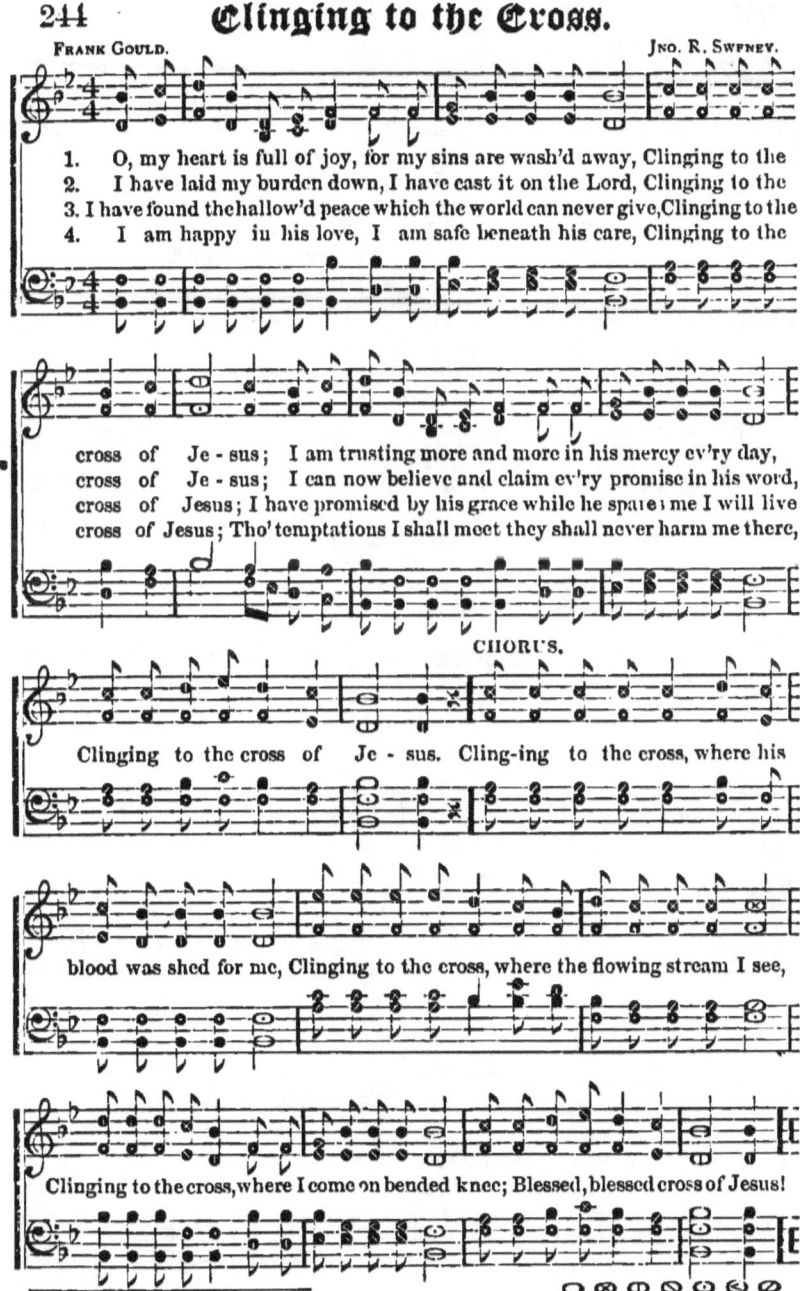

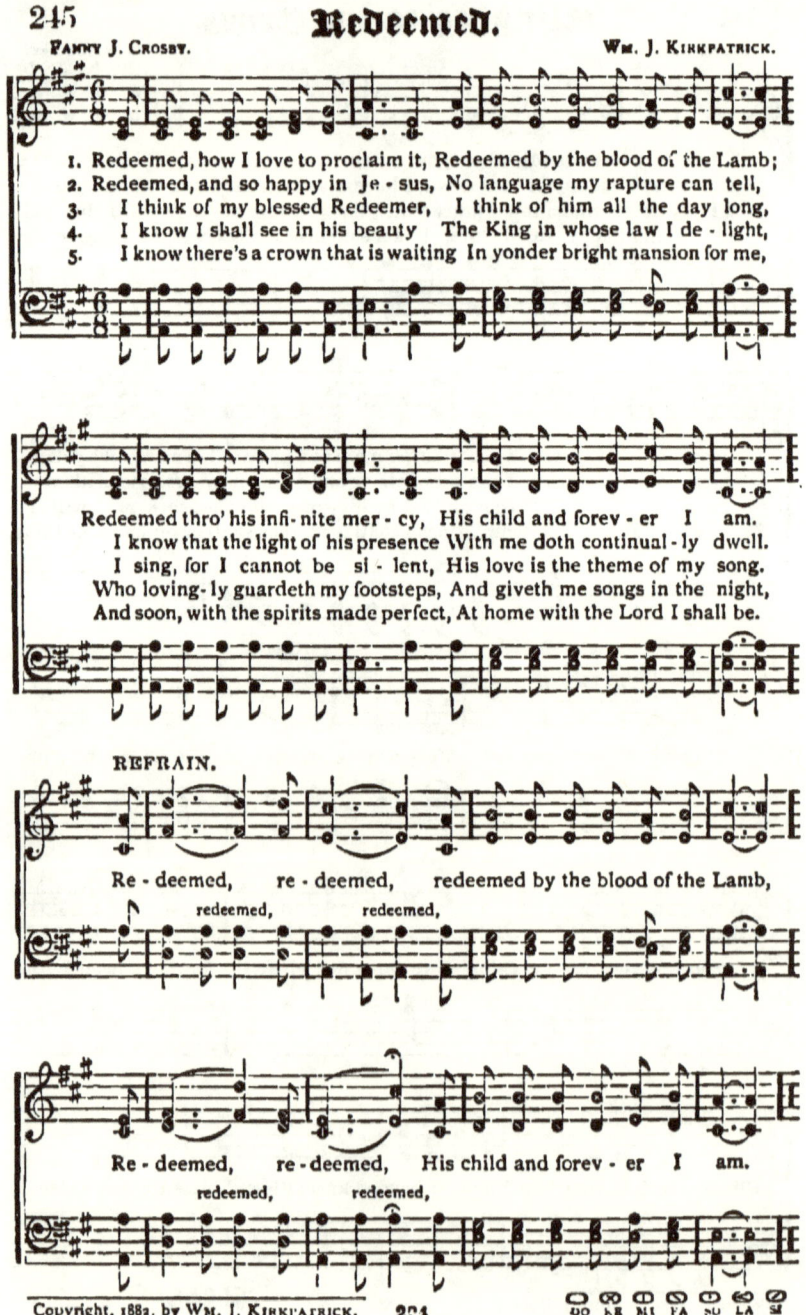

251. Rest.

Rev E. H. Stokes, D. D.
Jno. R. Sweney.

With feeling.

1. Touch my spir-it with thy Spir-it, Lord of All, my Sav-iour;
2. I have found him, what a treasure!—Found my blessed Sav-iour;
3. I have found him: past my weeping, Blessed, bles-sed Sav-iour;

Let me thy sweet rest in-her-it, This my high-est fa-vor.
This the pleasure of all pleasures, Rest in my dear Sav-iour.
And my soul to thy kind keep-ing I com-mit, dear Sav-iour.

CHORUS.

Rest, sweet rest, rest, sweet rest In my bles-sed Sav-iour;

Rest, sweet rest, rest, sweet rest In my bles-sed Sav-iour.

4 On the earth this heavenly resting
Comes to me, dear Saviour;
This is love's own manifesting,
Through my blessed Saviour.

5 In this rest toil does not weary,—
Toil for thee, my Saviour;
In the gloom there's nothing dreary,
With thee, O my Saviour.

Copyright, 1885, by John J. Hood.

252 **Praise the Lord.**

W. P. MACKAY, M. A.
With spirit.
P. G. FITHIAN.

1. Praise the Lord with hearts and voices, Gathered in his ho-ly name;
2. Praise the liv-ing God who gave us, Lost and ru-ined as we lay,
3. Praise him; en-e-mies as-sail us, As we through the desert go,

Ev-'ry quickened soul re-joic-es, Hear-ing of the Saviour's fame.
His be-lov-ed Son to save us, Bear-ing all our sin a-way.
But his sword can nev-er fail us, It shall si-lence ev-'ry foe.

CHORUS.

Praise the Lord, oh, praise him ev-er, Let our voic-es sweet-ly sing;

Praise the Lord! oh, may we ev-er Sing a-loud to God our King.

4 Praise him for the water flowing
   Freely in its boundless tide;
   Christ the smitten rock we're knowing,
   Praise him for his wounded side.

5 Praise him, thro' the desert marching,
   Onward to the golden shore;
   For our Saviour we are watching,
   And we'll praise him evermore.

Copyright, 1885, by JOHN J. HOOD.

4 Thus might I hide my blushing face
   While his dear cross appears,
   Dissolve my heart in thankfulness,
   And melt mine eyes to tears

5 But drops of grief can ne'er repay
   The debt of love I owe
   Here, Lord, I give myself away,—
   'Tis all that I can do.

259. Trusting in His Word.

"Verily, verily, I say unto you, He that heareth my word, and believeth on him that sent me, hath everlasting life."—John v. 24.

W. H. G. W. H. Geistweit.

1. I am trusting in the prom-ise Of the Saviour's blessed word;
2. I am cry-ing, "Ab-ba Fa-ther," For the promise I be-lieve,
3. From my sins for-ev-er turn-ing, I receive thee now, O Lord;
4. Ho-ly Spir-it, gracious Wit-ness, Make the word all power to me;

I am saved from all my vile-ness Through the merits of his blood.
If from sin I turn, and trust him, Endless life I then re-ceive.
I will fol-low, love, and serve thee, Resting whol-ly on thy word.
I am trust-ing, ful-ly trust-ing, I am now from sin set free.

CHORUS.

I am saved; oh, wondrous sto - ry! I am saved thro' Je-sus' blood;

I am saved; I'm ful-ly rest-ing On the promise of his word.

Copyright, 1885, by John J Hood.

264. We'll Know Each Other.

Mrs. E. C. Ellsworth. [From "The Wells of Salvation," by per.] Wm. J. Kirkpatrick.

1. Oh, we'll meet, and know each other, In the light of full-orbed day,
2. Wrongs that have our hearts withholden Stand aghast when light they see,
3. Oh, that bright and last up-lifting Of the mists which hide the true!
4. O that faith might nev-er waver, O that love would long for-bear,

Where the splendors of the morning Chase the shadows all a-way.
Doubts that have a brother questioned, There be-fore the day-light flee.
Heart to heart shall quickly answer When our love is stirred a-new.
Hope should point to yonder meet-ing, Per-fect love and trust are there.

CHORUS.

Yes, we'll meet, and know each other, Griefs no more shall hidden lie,

Bro-ther grasp the hand of brother, Face to face and eye to eye.

Copyright, 1881, by John J. Hood.

The Summer Land.—CONCLUDED.

hail   joy's eternal mor - row When the toils of earth shall cease, There to
There, there to hail,   there, there to hail,
song,   listen to the cho - rus," Praise the Lord the King of kings: Saved by
Hark, hark the song   hark, hark the song,
light   soon the sky adorn - ing We shall meet with joyful eyes; We shall
Pure holy light,   pure ho - ly light,

dwell   by the crystal riv - er, Blessed riv - er, blessed riv - er,
There, there to dwell,   there, there to dwell,   there, there to dwell,   there, there to dwell,
grace;   glory! halle - lu - jah! Halle - lu - jah! halle - lu - jah!
Saved, saved by grace,   saved, saved by grace,   saved, saved by grace,   saved, saved by grace,
meet   by the crystal riv - er, Shining riv - er, shining riv - er,
Yes, we shall meet,   yes, we shall meet,   yes, we shall meet,   yes, we shall meet,

With the Lord   happy and for- ev - er, When the toils of earth shall cease.
Dwell with the Lord,   dwell with the Lord,
Crowned with love; glory! halle - lu - jah! Praise the mighty King of kings."
Crowned, crowned with love,   crowned, crowned with love,
On its banks   meet no more to sev - er, Look beyond with joyful eyes.
There on its banks,   there on its banks,

270   F. J. C.   **The Prince of Peace.**   Tune above.

1 'Twas a night of long ago when all were
    sleeping, sleeping, sleeping, [keeping,
When the lonely silent stars a watch were
Softly o'er the dreaming, dreaming earth;
Floods of light bursting forth in glory,
    (Pure floods of light, pure floods of light, etc.,)
    Brightest glory, brightest glory,
Harp and voice told the joyful story
    (Sweet harp and voice, sweet harp and voice,)
    Of his birth the Prince of Peace.

Cho.—He has come; hail the lovely stranger,
    (Yes, he has come, yes, he has come, etc.,)
    Lovely stranger, lovely stranger;
Lo, the babe cradled in a manger
    (O blessed babe, O blessed babe,)
    Is the King and Prince of Peace.

2 See the rosy blushing morn again is
    breaking, breaking, breaking,
And the melody of song again is waking
    Music in the hearts of all to day;
Praise the Lord, come with happy voices,
    (Praise, praise the Lord, praise, praise the Lord,)
    Happy voices, happy voices,
Praise the Lord, how the world rejoices,
    (Praise, praise the Lord, praise, praise the Lord,)
    At his birth the Prince of Peace.

3 Hark the merry silver bells are sweetly
    ringing, ringing, ringing,
And the multitude of angels now are singing
    Glory in the highest evermore;
Sing aloud, glory! hallelujah!
    (Sing, sing aloud, sing, sing aloud, etc.,)
    Hallelujah! hallelujah!
Sing aloud, glory! hallelujah!
    (Sing, sing aloud, sing, sing aloud,)
    At his birth the Prince of Peace.

From "Hoed's Carols for—245—Christmas, No. 6," by per.

271. Soldiers of the Cross.

I. WATTS.   T. C. O'KANE.

1. Am I a sol-dier of the cross,— A foll'wer of the Lamb,— And shall I fear to own his cause, Or blush to speak his name?
2. Must I be car-ried to the skies On flowery beds of ease; While others fought to win the prize, And sailed thro' bloody seas?
3. Are there no foes for me to face? Must I not stem the flood? Is this vile world a friend to grace, To help me on to God.

CHORUS.

The conflict's be-fore us and we must a-rise, To battle for Jesus, his hon-or defend; As-sured of a mansion and crown in the skies, If faithful unto the end.

4 Sure I must fight if I would reign;
   Increase my courage, Lord!
   I'll bear the toil, endure the pain,
   Supported by thy word.
	5 Thy saints in all this glorious war
	   Shall conquer though they die:
	   They see the triumph from afar,—
	   By faith they bring it nigh.

Copyright, 1885, by T. C. O'KANE.

272. The Countersign.

NOTE.—George H. Stuart, Pres. U. S. Christian Commission, coming from a battle-field, was halted by a picket-guard and ordered to give the countersign. Giving the wrong word he was compelled to return to headquarters. Coming back, and giving the correct word, the guard shouted, "All right, pass on!" Mr. Stuart then asked, "Sentinel, have you *the* countersign?" "Yes." "What is it?" "The blood of Jesus."

Rev. Jno. O. Foster, A. M.
Jno. R. Sweney.

1. In the darkness, as I trod On a wayward, lost de-sign,
2. Trav-'ler, halt! where now you stand There is drawn a dead - ly line;
3. Back to where the words were given, There I sought the love di-vine;

Sud-den-ly a man of God Shout-ed for the coun-ter-sign.
Ere you pass to yon-der land You must give the coun-ter-sign.
When the order came from heaven, "Christ shall be your coun-ter-sign."

CHORUS.

Pass the word from soul to soul, Let it ring a-long the line:

"Je-sus Christ has made me whole!" This shall be my coun-ter-sign.

4 Sentinel, have you the word
  Given from thy God to thee?
Yes, I know the blessed Lord,
  "Th'-blood of Jesus" cleanseth me.

5 Guards will not arrest me now,
  Nothing's wrong within the line;
Heaven's light is on my brow,—
  Christ withing the countersign.

Copyright, 1884, by John J. Hood.

274. The Lord's Prayer. Matt. vi. — GREGORIAN.

Our Father, who art in heaven, | hallowed | be thy | name; ‖ Thy kingdom come,
  Thy will be done on | earth, : as it | is in | heaven;
Give us this | day our | daily | bread; ‖ And forgive us our debts, as | we for- |
  give our | debtors.
And lead us not into temptation, but de- | liver | us from | evil; ‖ For thine is
  the kingdom, and the power, and the glory, for- | ever. | A - | men.

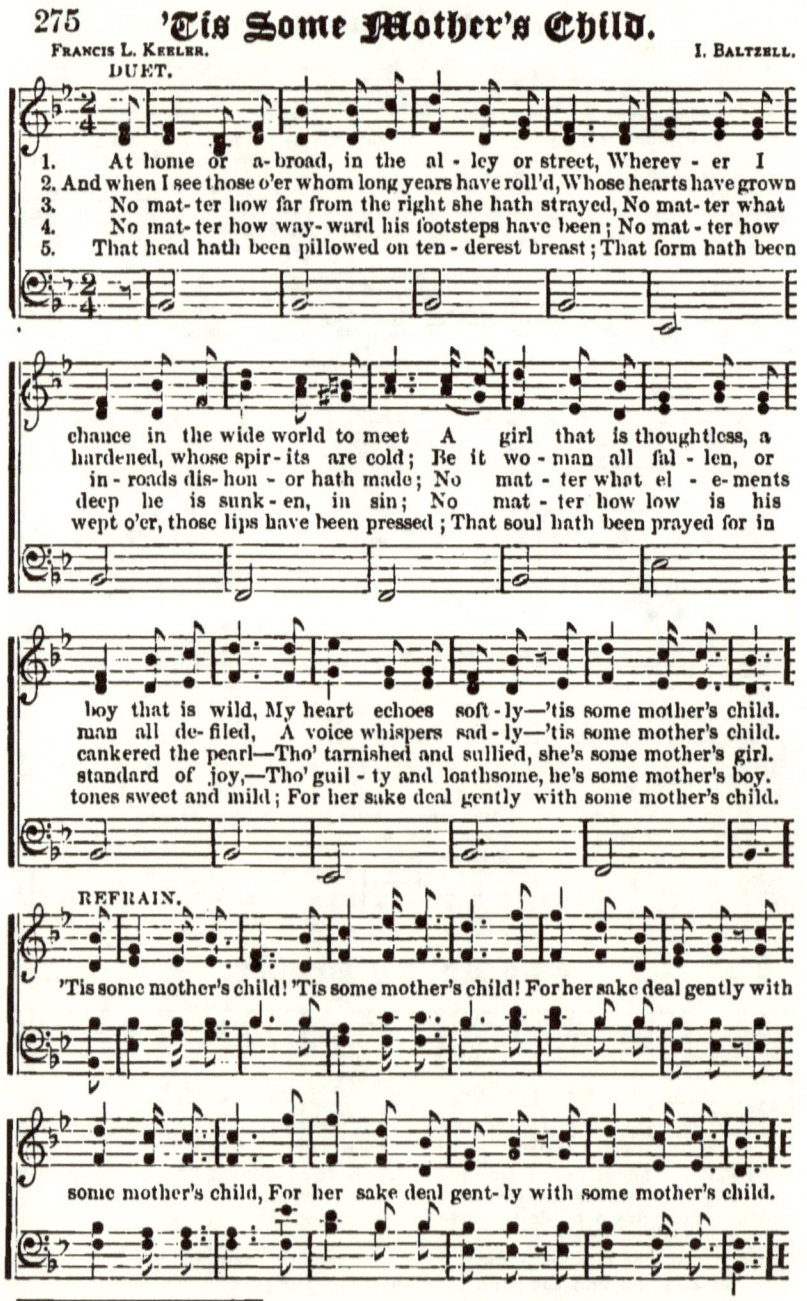

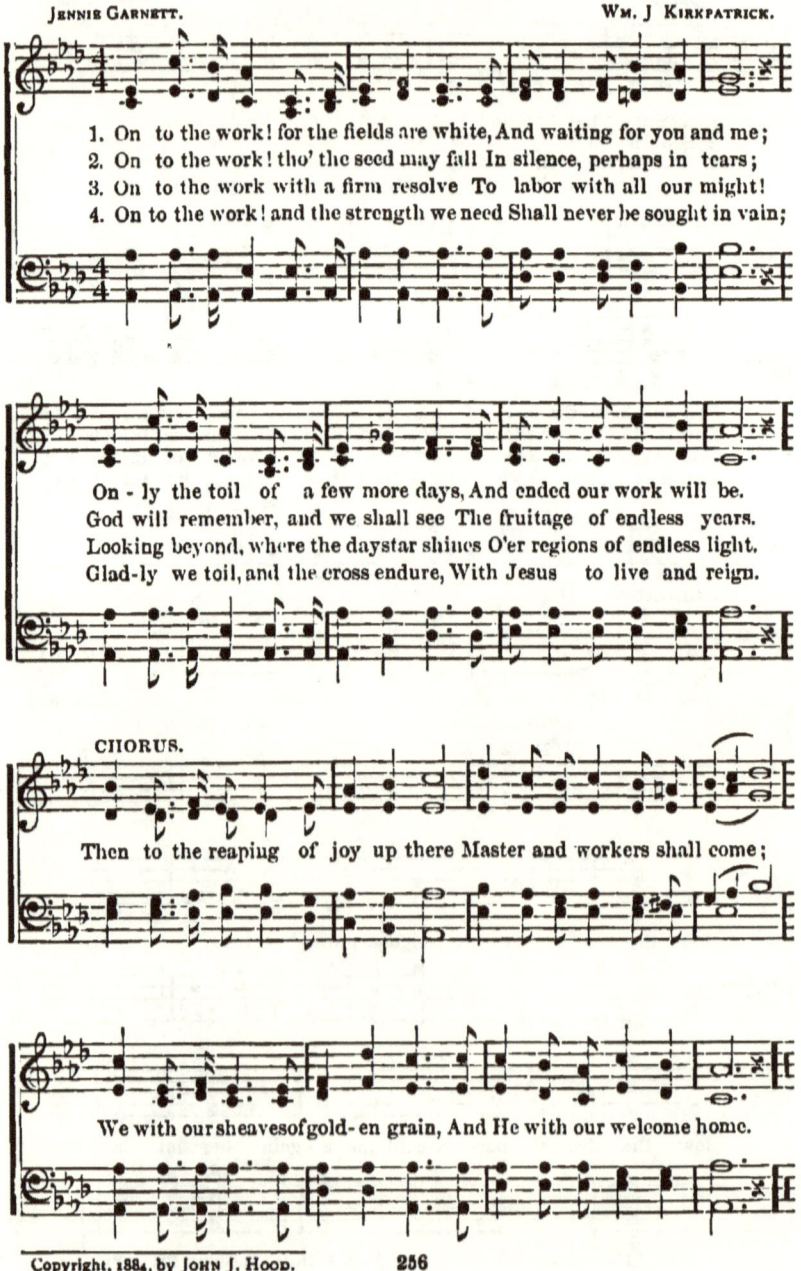

278. Oh, Where are the Reapers?

EBEN E. REXFORD.
GEO. F. ROOT.

Moderato.

1. Oh, where are the reap-ers that gar-ner in The sheaves of the good from the fields of sin; With sickles of truth must the work be done, And no one may rest till the "harvest home."
2. Go out in the by-ways and search them all; The wheat may be there, tho' the weeds are tall; Then search in the highway, and pass none by, But gath-er from all for the home on high.
3. The fields all are ripe-ning, and far and wide The world now is wait-ing the harvest-tide: But reapers are few, and the work is great, And much will be lost should the harvest wait.
4. So come with your sick-les, ye sons of men, And gath-er to-geth-er the gold-en grain; Toil on till the Lord of the harvest come, Then share ye his joy in the "harvest home."

CHORUS.

Where are the reapers! oh, who will come And share in the glo-ry of the "harvest home?" Oh, who will help us to gar-ner in The sheaves of good from the fields of sin?

By permission.   257   Temple Trio—R

279 **We are Going.**

Rev. Jno. O. Foster, A. M.
Jno. R. Sweney.

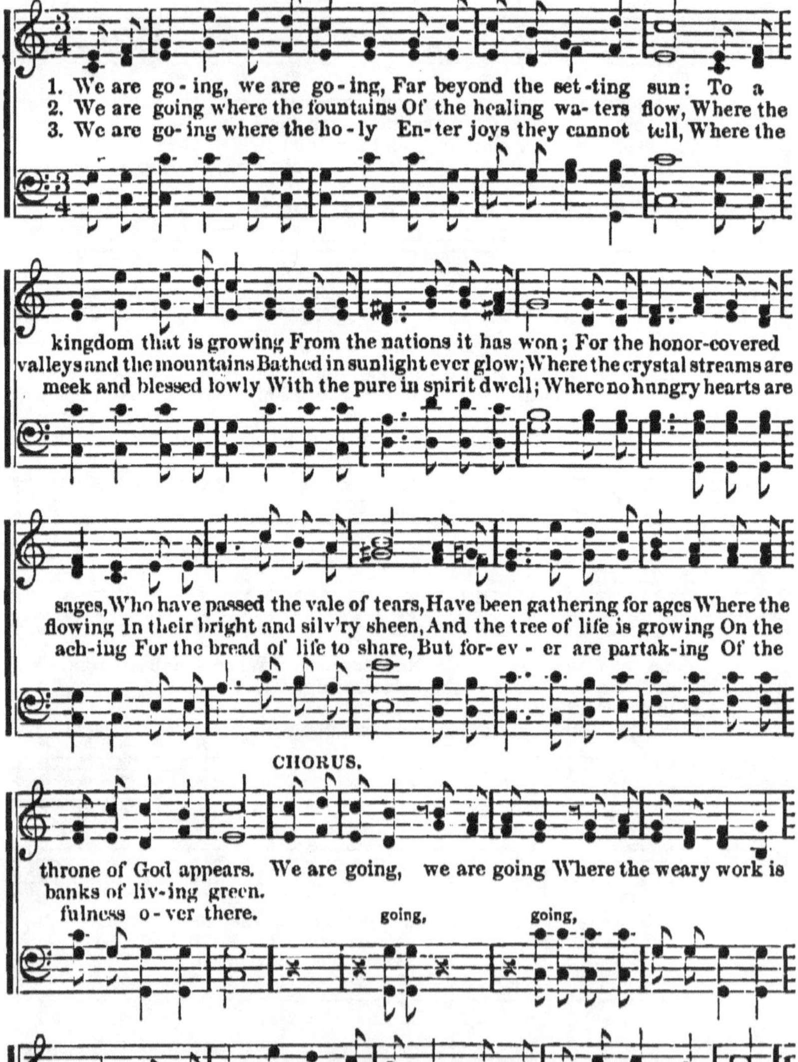

1. We are go-ing, we are go-ing, Far beyond the set-ting sun: To a kingdom that is growing From the nations it has won; For the honor-covered sages, Who have passed the vale of tears, Have been gathering for ages Where the throne of God appears.

2. We are going where the fountains Of the healing wa-ters flow, Where the valleys and the mountains Bathed in sunlight ever glow; Where the crystal streams are flowing In their bright and silv'ry sheen, And the tree of life is growing On the banks of liv-ing green.

3. We are go-ing where the ho-ly En-ter joys they cannot tell, Where the meek and blessed lowly With the pure in spirit dwell; Where no hungry hearts are ach-ing For the bread of life to share, But for-ev-er are partak-ing Of the fulness o-ver there.

CHORUS.

We are going, we are going Where the weary work is o'er, Where the morning light is glowing On the blessed, sun-ny shore.

Copyright, 1884, by John J. Hood.

The Lily of the Valley.

English Melody, arranged for this work.

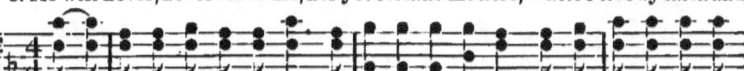

1. I have found a friend in Jesus, he's ev'rything to me, He's the fairest of ten
2. He all my griefs has taken, and all my sorrows borne; In temptation he's my
3. He will never, never leave me, nor yet forsake me here, While I live by faith and

thousand to my soul; The Li-ly of the Valley, in him alone I see All I
strong and mighty tower; I have all for him forsaken, and all my idols torn From my
do his blessed will; A wall of fire about me, I've nothing now to fear; With his

D. S.—Lily of the Valley, the bright and Morning Star, He's the

Fine.

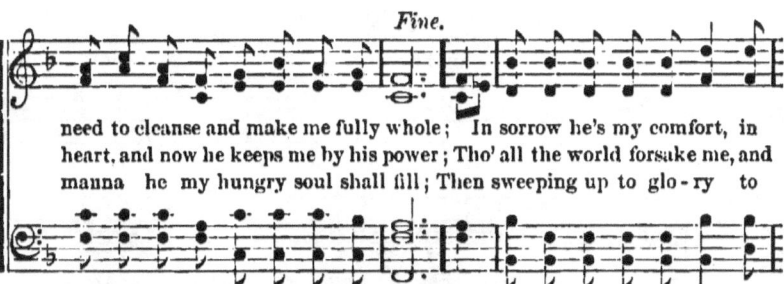

need to cleanse and make me fully whole; In sorrow he's my comfort, in
heart, and now he keeps me by his power; Tho' all the world forsake me, and
manna he my hungry soul shall fill; Then sweeping up to glo-ry to

fair-est of ten thousand to my soul. CHO.—In sorrow, etc. (*after each verse.*)

D. S.

trouble he's my stay, He tells me ev'ry care on him to roll.   He's the
Satan tempts me sore, Thro' Jesus I shall safely reach the goal.   He's the
see his blessed face, Where rivers of delight shall ever roll.   He's the

Copyright, 1885, by JOHN J. HOOD.

283. Can you do without Him?

"Without me ye can do nothing."—John xv. 5.

Mrs. E. W. Chapman.   Chas. Edw. Prior.

Slowly.

1. Can you do without the Saviour, Tend'rer far than human friend?
2. Can you do without the Saviour When the last loud trump shall sound?
3. Can you do without the Saviour, With the el-ements a-flame?

When this poor, weak frame with anguish Direst pain and sor-row rend?
When th'entomb-ed millions gath-er, And the judgment seat surround?
When the voice of God like thunder Shall in wrath pronounce your name?

CHORUS.

Can you, can you do without him? Shall you not his pi-ty need?

Trembling sin-ner, can you, can you Do without this Friend indeed?

Copyright, 1885, by John J. Hood.

287. Make Room for Me.

Jamie S——, a most wonderful violinist at the age of eight, was withal a very frail child. One afternoon after playing at a matinee, he fainted, and was carried home in his father's arms. He was also engaged to play that night in another place, but was urged to remain at home, on account of his extreme weakness; but he pleaded with his father until he was again in the music hall. Returning he lay down to sleep, with his father by his side. Thinking his boy comfortable for the night the father, too, retired. Very soon he heard his boy saying, softly, "Lord Jesus, make room in heaven for a little boy like me." When morning came the father found that "room" had been made for his child, for Jamie had passed out, and up, and in!

W. H. G.   W. H. Geistweit.

1. A lit-tle boy lay down to rest Close by his fa-ther's side,
2. The fa-ther heard the sim-ple prayer And closely held his boy,
3. The Saviour heard his yearning plea, And sent an an-gel down

And dreamed of heaven, that city fair, Whose gate stands open wide;
When o'er his face a light broke forth Of heaven's last-ing joy;
To tell the child to en-ter in, And take his gold-en crown;

He saw the Saviour's lov-ing face, He oft had longed to see,
No oth-er words came from his heart Save these, said earnest-ly,
Up through the sky he sped his way To yon-der ci-ty fair,

While from his lips went forth a prayer, "Make room in heaven for me."
"Dear, blessed Lord, make room in heaven For-a little boy like me."
And found, indeed, a room in heaven, For-ev-er his,—up there.

Copyright, 1885, by John J. Hood.

Make Room for Me.—CONCLUDED.

Make room for me, Lord Je-sus, Make room in heaven for me; Hast thou not room up yon-der, Lord, For a lit-tle boy like me?

288 ### I'll Live for Him.

C. R. Dunbar.

1. My life, my love   I give to thee, Thou Lamb of God, who died for me;
2. I now believe thou dost receive, For thou hast died that I might live;
3. Oh, thou who died on Cal-va-ry, To save my soul and make me free,

Cho.—I'll live for him who died for me, How happy then my life shall be!

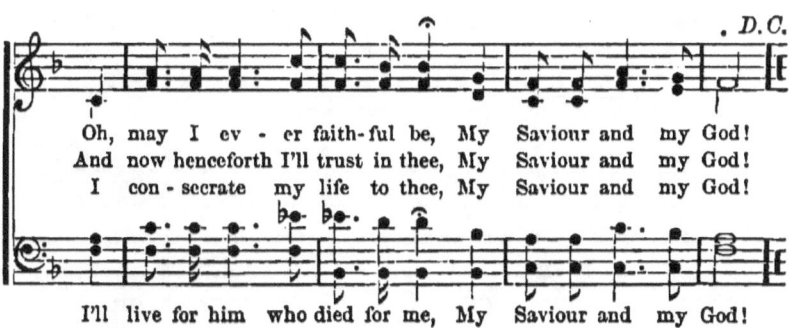

Oh, may I ev-er faith-ful be, My Saviour and my God!
And now henceforth I'll trust in thee, My Saviour and my God!
I con-secrate my life to thee, My Saviour and my God!

I'll live for him who died for me, My Saviour and my God!

By permission.

291. Step out upon the Promises.

AMELIA M. STARKWEATHER. JNO. R. SWENEY.

Moderato.

1. Has the day been dark with shadows, And the evening shut you
   Has the day been dark with shadows, Has the day been dark with shadows,
2. Are you tempted and discouraged? Do the trials of the
3. If you follow in His foot-steps, You can never go a-
4. As the stars that in the heavens Look like diamonds in the

in, shut you in, Full of bitter disappointment For the
Full of bitter disappointment, Full of bitter disappointment,
hour of the hour Like a flood sweep in upon you With an
stray, go astray, Tho' it be across the desert, He went
night, in the night, So his promises shine brightest When we

place you hoped to win? *hoped to win?* Then step out upon this promise, For his
overwhelming power? *mighty power?* Then step out upon this promise; It was
all that lonely way; *lonely way;* Then step out upon this promise, On his
cannot see the light; *see the light;* Then step out upon this promise Of your

word is good and true: "If you love the blessed Master, All things work for good to you;"
tried by one of old: "I'll be with thee in all trouble, And will bring thee forth as gold;"
word you may rely: "In the right way I'll instruct thee, I will guide thee with mine eye;"
best and truest friend: "I will never, never leave thee; I'll be with thee to the end;"

Copyright, 1885, by JOHN J. HOOD.

Step out upon the Promises.—CONCLUDED.

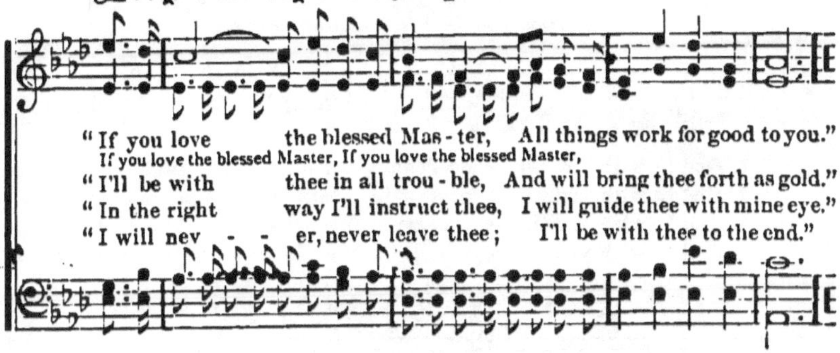

"If you love the blessed Mas-ter, All things work for good to you."
If you love the blessed Master, If you love the blessed Master,
"I'll be with thee in all trou-ble, And will bring thee forth as gold."
"In the right way I'll instruct thee, I will guide thee with mine eye."
"I will nev - - er, never leave thee; I'll be with thee to the end."

292. Glory to His Name.

Rev. E. A. Hoffman. "I will glorify thy name forevermore." Rev. J. H. Stockton.

1. Down at the cross where my Saviour died, Down where for cleansing from
2. I am so won-drously sav'd from sin, Je-sus so sweetly a-
3. Oh, precious fountain, that saves from sin, I am so glad I have
4. Come to this fountain, so rich and sweet; Cast thy poor soul at the

sin I cried; There to my heart was the blood applied; Glory to his
bides with-in; There at the cross where he took me in; Glo-ry to his
entered in; There Je-sus saves me and keeps me clean, Glory to his
Saviour's feet; Plunge in to-day, and be made complete; Glo-ry to his

D.S.—There to my heart was the blood applied; Glo-ry to his

Fine. CHORUS. *D.S.*

name. Glo-ry to his name, Glo-ry to his name;

By permission. 271

DO RE MI FA SO LA SI

Ariel. C. P. M. Arr. by Lowell Mason.

295 O Love Divine.

1 O LOVE divine, how sweet thou art!
  When shall I find my willing heart
    All taken up by thee?
  I thirst, I faint, I die to prove
  The greatness of redeeming love,
    The love of Christ to me.

2 Stronger his love than death or hell!
  Its riches are unsearchable;
    The first-born sons of light
  Desire in vain its depths to see;
  They cannot reach the mystery,
    The length, the breadth, the height.

3 God only knows the love of God;
  O that it now were shed abroad
    In this poor stony heart!
  For love I sigh, for love I pine;
  This only portion, Lord, be mine;
    Be mine this better part.

4 O that I could forever sit
  With Mary at the Master's feet!
    Be this my happy choice;
  My only care, delight, and bliss,
  My joy, my heaven on earth, be this,
    To hear the Bridegroom's voice.

5 O that I could, with favored John,
  Recline my weary head upon
    The dear Redeemer's breast!
  From care, and sin, and sorrow free,
  Give me, O Lord, to find in thee
    My everlasting rest.

296 O could I Speak.

1 O COULD I speak the matchless worth,
  O could I sound the glories forth,
    Which in my Saviour shine,
  I'd soar and touch the heavenly strings,
  And vie with Gabriel while he sings
    In notes almost divine.

2 I'd sing the precious blood he spilt,
  My ransom from the dreadful guilt
    Of sin, and wrath divine;
  I'd sing his glorious righteousness,
  In which all-perfect, heavenly dress
    My soul shall ever shine.

3 I'd sing the characters he bears,
  And all the forms of love he wears,
    Exalted on his throne;
  In loftiest songs of sweetest praise,
  I would to everlasting days
    Make all his glories known.

4 Well, the delightful day will come
  When my dear Lord will bring me home,
    And I shall see his face;
  Then with my Saviour, Brother, Friend,
  A blest eternity I'll spend,
    Triumphant in his grace.

Luther. S. M.

Dr. T. Hastings.

297   I love Thy kingdom.

1 I LOVE thy kingdom, Lord,
   The house of thine abode,
The Church our blest Redeemer saved
   With his own precious blood.

2 I love thy Church, O God!
   Her walls before thee stand,
Dear as the apple of thine eye,
   And graven on thy hand.

3 For her my tears shall fall,
   For her my prayers ascend:
To her my cares and toils be given,
   Till toils and cares shall end.

4 Beyond my highest joy
   I prize her heavenly ways,
Her sweet communion, solemn vows,
   Her hymns of love and praise.

5 Sure as thy truth shall last,
   To Zion shall be given
The brightest glories earth can yield,
   And brighter bliss of heaven.

298   Grace!

1 GRACE! 'tis a charming sound,
   Harmonious to the ear;
Heaven with the echo shall resound,
   And all the earth shall hear.

2 Grace first contrived a way
   To save rebellious man;
And all the steps that grace display,
   Which drew the wondrous plan.

3 Grace taught my roving feet
   To tread the heavenly road;
And new supplies each hour I meet,
   While pressing on to God.

4 Grace all the work shall crown
   Through everlasting days;
It lays in heaven the topmost stone,
   And well deserves our praise.

299   Stand up, and bless.

1 STAND up, and bless the Lord,
   Ye people of his choice;
Stand up, and bless the Lord your God,
   With heart, and soul, and voice.

2 Though high above all praise,
   Above all blessing high,
Who would not fear his holy name,
   And laud, and magnify?

3 O for the living flame
   From his own altar brought,
To touch our lips, our souls inspire,
   And wing to heaven our thought!

4 God is our strength and song,
   And his salvation ours;
Then be his love in Christ proclaimed
   With all our ransomed powers.

5 Stand up, and bless the Lord;
   The Lord your God adore;
Stand up, and bless his glorious name,
   Henceforth, forevermore.

300   Purity of heart.

1 BLEST are the pure in heart,
   For they shall see our God;
The secret of the Lord is theirs;
   Their soul is his abode.

2 Still to the lowly soul
   He doth himself impart,
And for his temple and his throne
   Selects the pure in heart.

3 Lord, we thy presence seek,
   May ours this blessing be;
O give the pure and lowly heart,—
   A temple meet for thee.

Doxology. S. M.

To God, the Father, Son,
   And Spirit, One in Three,
Be glory, as it was, is now,
   And shall forever be.

Zerah. C. M. Dr. L. Mason.

301   Come, ye that love.

1 COME, ye that love the Saviour's name,
   And joy to make it known,
   The Sovereign of your hearts proclaim,
   And bow before his throne.

2 Behold your Lord, your Master crowned
   With glories all divine;
   And tell the wondering nations round
   How bright those glories shine.

3 When, in his earthly courts, we view
   The glories of our King,
   We long to love as angels do,
   And wish like them to sing.

4 And shall we long and wish in vain?
   Lord. teach our songs to rise:
   Thy love can animate the strain,
   And bid it reach the skies.

302   What glory gilds.

1 WHAT glory gilds the sacred page!
   Majestic, like the sun,
   It gives a light to every age;
   It gives, but borrows none.

2 The power that gave it still supplies
   The gracious light and heat;
   Its truths upon the nations rise;
   They rise, but never set.

3 Lord, everlasting thanks be thine
   For such a bright display,
   As makes a world of darkness shine
   With beams of heavenly day.

4 My soul rejoices to pursue
   The steps of him I love,
   Till glory breaks upon my view
   In brighter worlds above.

303   The Prince of Peace.

1 To us a Child of hope is born,
   To us a Son is given;
   Him shall the tribes of earth obey,
   Him, all the hosts of heaven.

2 His name shall be the Prince of Peace,
   Forevermore adored;
   The Wonderful, the Counselor,
   The great and mighty Lord.

3 His power, increasing, still shall spread;
   His reign no end shall know;
   Justice shall guard his throne above,
   And peace abound below.

4 To us a Child of hope is born,
   To us a Son is given;
   The Wonderful, the Counselor,
   The mighty Lord of heaven.

304   The joyful sound.

1 SALVATION! O the joyful sound
   What pleasure to our ears!
   A sovereign balm for every wound,
   A cordial for our fears.

2 Salvation! let the echo fly
   The spacious earth around,
   While all the armies of the sky
   Conspire to raise the sound.

3 Salvation! O thou bleeding Lamb!
   To thee the praise belongs:
   Salvation shall inspire our hearts,
   And dwell upon our tongues.

Doxology. C. M.

To Father, Son, and Holy Ghost,
   The God whom we adore,
Be glory, as it was, is now,
   And shall be evermore.

Antioch. C. M.

305 O for a thousand tongues.

1 O FOR a thousand tongues, to sing
   My great Redeemer's praise;
   The glories of my God and King,
   The triumphs of his grace!

2 My gracious Master and my God,
   Assist me to proclaim,
   To spread through all the earth abroad,
   The honors of thy name.

3 Jesus! the name that charms our fears,
   That bids our sorrows cease;
   'Tis music in the sinner's ears,
   'Tis life, and health, and peace.

4 He breaks the power of canceled sin,
   He sets the prisoner free;
   His blood can make the foulest clean;
   His blood availed for me.

5 He speaks, and, listening to his voice,
   New life the dead receive;
   The mournful, broken hearts rejoice;
   The humble poor believe.

6 Hear him, ye deaf; his praise, ye dumb,
   Your loosened tongues employ;
   Ye blind, behold your Saviour come;
   And leap, ye lame, for joy.

306 Joy to the world!

1 JOY to the world! the Lord is come;
   Let earth receive her King;
   Let every heart prepare him room,
   And heaven and nature sing.

2 Joy to the world! the Saviour reigns;
   Let men their songs employ;
   While fields and floods, rocks, hills and
   Repeat the sounding joy.   [plains,

3 No more let sin and sorrow grow,
   Nor thorns infest the ground;
   He comes to make his blessings flow
   Far as the curse is found.

4 He rules the world with truth and grace,
   And makes the nations prove
   The glories of his righteousness,
   And wonders of his love.

307 Evils of Intemperance. Tune, BOYLSTON.

1 MOURN for the thousands slain,
   The youthful and the strong;
   Mourn for the wine-cup's fearful reign,
   And the deluded throng.

2 Mourn for the ruined soul—
   Eternal life and light
   Lost by the fiery, maddening bowl,
   And turned to hopeless night.

3 Mourn for the lost,—but call,
   Call to the strong, the free;
   Rouse them to shun that dreadful fall,
   And to the refuge flee.

4 Mourn for the lost,—but pray,
   Pray to our God above,
   To break the fell destroyer's sway,
   And show his saving love.

308 What Ruin! Tune, EVAN.

1 WHAT ruin hath intemperance wrought!
   How widely roll its waves!
   How many myriads hath it brought
   To fill dishonored graves!

2 And see, O Lord, what numbers still
   Are maddened by the bowl,
   Led captive at the tyrant's will
   In bondage, heart and soul.

3 Stretch forth thy hand, O God, our King,
   And break the galling chain;
   Deliverance to the captive bring,
   And end the usurper's reign.

4 The cause of temperance is thine own;
   Our plans and efforts bless;
   We trust, O Lord, in thee alone
   To crown them with success.

309 How happy every child.

1 How happy every child of grace,
    Who knows his sins forgiven!
  "This earth," he cries, "is not my place,
    I seek my place in heaven,—
  A country far from mortal sight;
    Yet O, by faith I see
  The land of rest, the saints' delight,
    The heaven prepared for me."

2 O what a blessed hope is ours!
    While here on earth we stay,
  We more than taste the heavenly
    And antedate that day;   [powers,
  We feel the resurrection near,
    Our life in Christ concealed,
  And with his glorious presence here
    Our earthen vessels filled.

3 O would he more of heaven bestow,
    And let the vessels break,
  And let our ransomed spirits go
    To grasp the God we seek;
  In rapturous awe on him to gaze,
    Who bought the sight for me;
  And shout and wonder at his grace
    Through all eternity!

310 I heard the voice of Jesus.

1 I HEARD the voice of Jesus say,
    "Come unto me and rest;
  Lay down, thou weary one, lay down
    Thy head upon my breast!"
  I came to Jesus as I was,
    Weary, and worn, and sad,
  I found in him a resting-place,
    And he hath made me glad.

2 I heard the voice of Jesus say,
    "Behold, I freely give
  The living water; thirsty one,
    Stoop down, and drink, and live!"
  I came to Jesus, and I drank
    Of that life-giving stream;
  My thirst was quenched, my soul re-
    And now I live in him.   [vived,

3 I heard the voice of Jesus say,
    "I am this dark world's light;
  Look unto me, thy morn shall rise
    And all thy day be bright!"
  I looked to Jesus, and I found
    In him my Star, my Sun;
  And in that light of life I'll walk,
    Till all my journey's done.

311 Work, for the night is coming.

1 WORK, for the night is coming,
    Work through the morning hours;
  Work, while the dew is sparkling,
    Work 'mid springing flowers;
  Work, when the day grows brighter,
    Work in the glowing sun;
  Work, for the night is coming,
    When man's work is done.

2 Work, for the night is coming,
    Work through the sunny noon;
  Fill brightest hours with labor,
    Rest comes sure and soon,
  Give every flying minute
    Something to keep in store:
  Work, for the night is coming,
    When man works no more.

3 Work, for the night is coming,
    Under the sunset skies;
  While their bright tints are glowing,
    Work, for daylight flies.
  Work till the last beam fadeth,
    Fadeth to shine no more;
  Work while the night is darkening,
    When man's work is o'er.

Hebron. L. M.
Dr. L. Mason.

312 Thus far the Lord hath led.

1 Thus far the Lord hath led me on,
Thus far his power prolongs my days;
And every evening shall make known
Some fresh memorial of his grace.

2 Much of my time has run to waste,
And I, perhaps, am near my home;
But he forgives my follies past,
And gives me strength for days to come.

3 I lay my body down to sleep;
Peace is the pillow for my head;
While well-appointed angels keep
Their watchful stations round my bed.

4 Thus, when the night of death shall come,
My flesh shall rest beneath the ground,
And wait thy voice to rouse my tomb,
With sweet salvation in the sound.

313 O that my load.

1 O that my load of sin were gone!
O that I could at last submit
At Jesus' feet to lay it down—
To lay my soul at Jesus' feet!

2 Rest for my soul I long to find:
Saviour of all, if mine thou art,
Give me thy meek and lowly mind,
And stamp thine image on my heart.

3 Break off the yoke of inbred sin,
And fully set my spirit free;
I cannot rest till pure within,
Till I am wholly lost in thee.

4 Fain would I learn of thee, my God,
Thy light and easy burden prove,
The cross, all stained with hallowed blood,
The labor of thy dying love. [blood,

5 I would, but thou must give the power;
My heart from every sin release;
Bring near, bring near the joyful hour,
And fill me with thy perfect peace.

314 Lord, I am thine.

1 Lord, I am thine, entirely thine,
Purchased and saved by blood divine;
With full consent thine I would be,
And own thy sov'reign right in me.

2 Grant one poor sinner more a place
Among the children of thy grace;
A wretched sinner, lost to God,
But ransomed by Immanuel's blood.

3 Thine would I live, thine would I die,
Be thine through all eternity;
The vow is past beyond repeal,
And now I set the solemn seal.

4 Here, at that cross where flows the blood
That bought my guilty soul for God,
Thee my new Master now I call,
And consecrate to thee my all.

5 Do thou assist a feeble worm
The great engagement to perform;
Thy grace can full assistance lend,
And on that grace I dare depend.

315 The pilgrims' song.

1 Children of the heavenly King,
As we journey let us sing;
Sing our Saviour's worthy praise,
Glorious in his works and ways.

2 We are traveling home to God,
In the way our fathers trod;
They are happy now, and we
Soon their happiness shall see.

3 O ye banished seed, be glad;
Christ our Advocate is made:
Us to save our flesh assumes,
Brother to our souls becomes.

4 Lift your eyes, ye sons of light;
Zion's city is in sight;
There our endless home shall be,
There our Lord we soon shall see.

5 Fear not, brethren, joyful stand
On the borders of our land;
Jesus Christ, our Father's Son,
Bids us undismayed go on.

6 Lord, obediently we'll go,
Gladly leaving all below;
Only thou our Leader be,
And we still will follow thee.

FOR

Times of Refreshing and Revival,

SELECTED BY

THOMAS HARRISON.

MUSICAL EDITORS:

Jno. R. Sweney and Wm. J. Kirkpatrick.

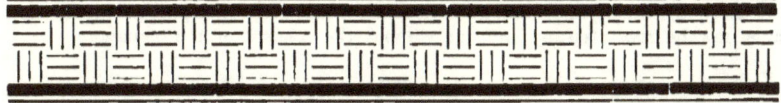

Philadelphia: JOHN J. HOOD, 1018 Arch St.

COPYRIGHT, 1885, BY JOHN J. HOOD.

AN experience of many years' work as a Revivalist has made manifest to me the desirableness of having a MUSIC edition of hymns contained in the smaller book of words only. In preparing the same I received the assistance as musical editors of Jno. R. Sweney, Mus. Doc., and Wm. J. Kirkpatrick. The valuable service rendered by these authors in the field of Christian song is widely recognised, and it is believed will recommend the musical department of PRECIOUS HYMNS to Gospel Singers generally.

THOS. HARRISON.

SPECIAL NOTICE.

Nearly all the hymns and music in this book are copyright property, they must not be reprinted by any one without the consent of the owners.

Precious Hymns.

317. He will Gather the Wheat.

HARRIET B. M'KEEVER.   JNO. R. SWENEY.

1. When Jesus shall gather the nations Before him at last to appear,
2. Shall we hear, from the lips of the Saviour, The words, 'Faithful servant, well done;'
3. He will smile when he looks on his children, And sees on the ransomed his seal;

Then, oh, how shall we stand in the judgment, When summoned our sentence to hear?
Or, trembling with fear and with anguish, Be banished away from his throne.
He will clothe them in heavenly beauty, As low at his footstool they kneel.

CHORUS.

He will gather the wheat in his garner, But the chaff will he scatter away;
Then, oh, how shall we stand in the judgment Of the great Resurrection Day?

4 Then let us be watching and waiting,—
Our lamps burning steady and bright,—
When the Bridegroom shall call to the wed-
Our spirits made ready for flight. [ding

5 Thus living with hearts fixed on heaven,
In patience we wait for the time,
When, the days of our pilgrimage ended,
We'll bask in the presence divine.

318. Hallelujah, He Saves Us.

FRANK M. DAVIS. [From "The Wells of Salvation," by per.] JNO. R. SWENEY.

1. Sing glo-ry to God in the highest, For wonderful things he hath done;
2. Oh, perfect redemption to sinners, The purchase of Jesus' own blood!
3. Rejoice, then, rejoice, all ye people, The wondrous transaction is done,

He so loved the world that he gave us His on-ly begot-ten dear Son.
The vil-est offend-er is pardoned, Is saved thro' the promise of God.
The life-gate is opened; come, enter, Thro' Je-sus the Cru-ci-fied One.

CHORUS.

Hal-le-lu - - jah! he saves us Thro' the death of his Son;
Hal-le-lu-jah!

Hal-le-lu - jah! he saves us Thro' the Cru-ci-fied One.
Hal-le-lu-jah!

Copyright, 1881, by JOHN J. HOOD.

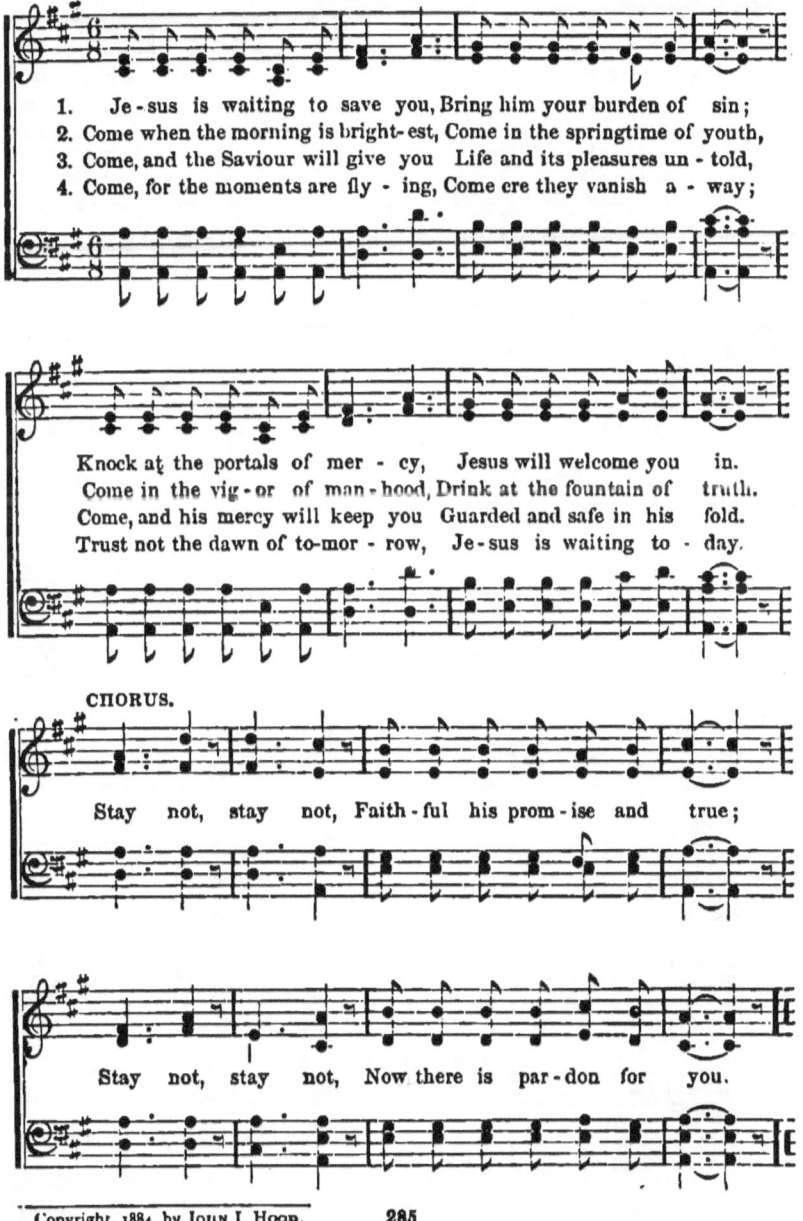

321. Lost but Found.

F. J. C. — Jno. R. Sweney.

1. Oh, the joy that fills my heart! Oh, the grateful tears that start, When I think of Jesus' love! How he came that he might bear All my weight of sin and care, How he came from heav'n above.

2. Lost but found, oh, wondrous thought! To his fold in mercy brought; Saved by grace, his grace divine; Heir with him of bliss untold, Soon his glory I'll behold, What a blessed hope is mine!

CHORUS.
Endless praise, endless praise To the Lord my soul shall raise;
Lost but found, O happy strain! Dead but now I live, but now I live again, live again.

3 Lost but found! I now can sing
Vict'ry through my Saviour King,
‖: Vict'ry ev'ry day and hour; :‖
Vict'ry still will be my song
When I join the ransom'd throng,
‖: Vict'ry o'er the tempter's power. :‖

4 O that all the world would prove
How a pard'ning God can love,
‖: How he waits for all who come! :‖
O that all the world might see
What his grace hath done for me!
‖: How he welcomes wand'rers home. :‖

COPYRIGHT, 1880, by JOHN J. HOOD.

322 **Only His Love.**

FANNY J. CROSBY. [From "The Wells of Salvation," by per.] WM. J. KIRKPATRICK.

1. Oh, to be near-er, near-er The feet of my Lord and King!
2. Oh, to be near-er, near-er, Communing with him in prayer!
3. Oh, to be near-er, near-er My Refuge, my Hope, my All!
4. Oh, for a faith still brighter, And clearer from day to day!

Oh, to en-joy his pres-ence, And on-ly his love to sing!
Oh, to be strong-er, strong-er, My bur-den of toil to bear!
Oh, to be al-ways read-y To an-swer my Sav-iour's call!
Oh, to be more like Je-sus, In all that I do and say!

CHORUS.

On-ly his love, on-ly his love, Ev-er my song shall be: His wonder-ful love, pre-par-ing a-bove A robe and a crown for me.

Copyright, 1881, by JOHN J. HOOD.

323. The Old Ship.

"The ship was now in the midst of the sea"—Matt. xiv. 24. T. C. O'Kane.

1. We are on the deep, we are sail-ing to our home In the land be-yond the shores of time, Where the wea-ry rest, and no sor-rows ev-er come, In that brighter, bet-ter, hap-pier clime.

2. We are on the deep, see our sails how full they swell, And our stand-ard float-ing proudly high; 'Tis the blood-stained banner of King Imman-u-el, We will sail beneath it—"live or die."

3. Are you on the deep, in the sin-ner's bark so frail? You will per-ish—leave without de-lay; Come on board with us, and at once for glo-ry sail, And be saved while you are called to-day.

D.S.—safe at an-chor ride, In the port on Canaan's peace-ful shore.

CHORUS.

In the old ship Zi-on we are sail-ing on the tide; Though the waves may dash, and billows roar, "We will stand the storm," we will

By permission.

Temple Trio—T

3 Can my lips be mute, or my heart be sad,
  When the gracious Master hath made me glad?
  When he points where the many mansions be,
  And sweetly says, 'There is one for thee'?

4 I shall catch the gleam of its jasper wall
  When I come to the gloom of the evenfall,
  For I know that the shadows, dreary and dim,
  Have a path of light that will lead to him.

From "Gems of Praise," by per.

325. Fill Me Now.

Rev. E. H. Stokes, D.D.   Jno. R. Sweney.

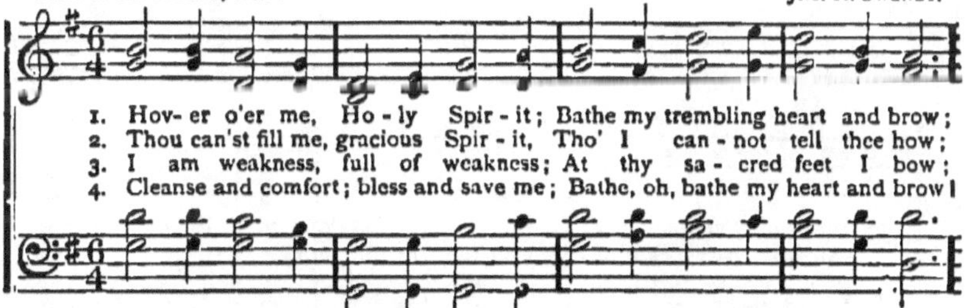

1. Hov-er o'er me, Ho-ly Spir-it; Bathe my trembling heart and brow;
2. Thou can'st fill me, gracious Spir-it, Tho' I can-not tell thee how;
3. I am weakness, full of weakness; At thy sa-cred feet I bow;
4. Cleanse and comfort; bless and save me; Bathe, oh, bathe my heart and brow

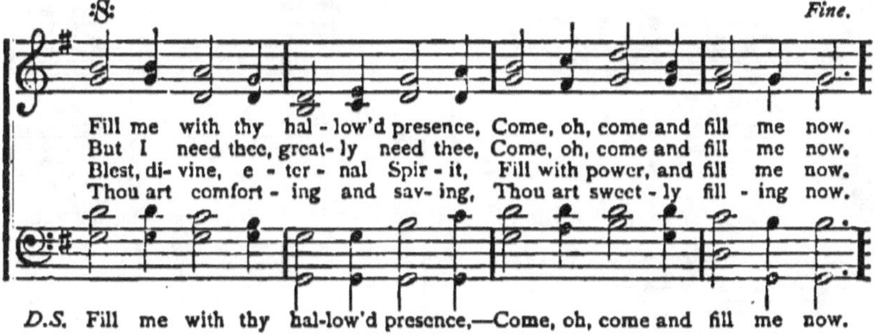

Fill me with thy hal-low'd presence, Come, oh, come and fill me now.
But I need thee, great-ly need thee, Come, oh, come and fill me now.
Blest, di-vine, e-ter-nal Spir-it, Fill with power, and fill me now.
Thou art comfort-ing and sav-ing, Thou art sweet-ly fill-ing now.

D.S. Fill me with thy hal-low'd presence,—Come, oh, come and fill me now.

Chorus.

Fill me now, fill me now, Je-sus, come, and fill me now;

Copyright, 1879, by John J. Hood.

Calling for You.

FANNY J. CROSBY. [From "The Wells of Salvation," by per.] WM. J. KIRKPATRICK.

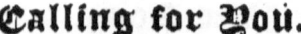

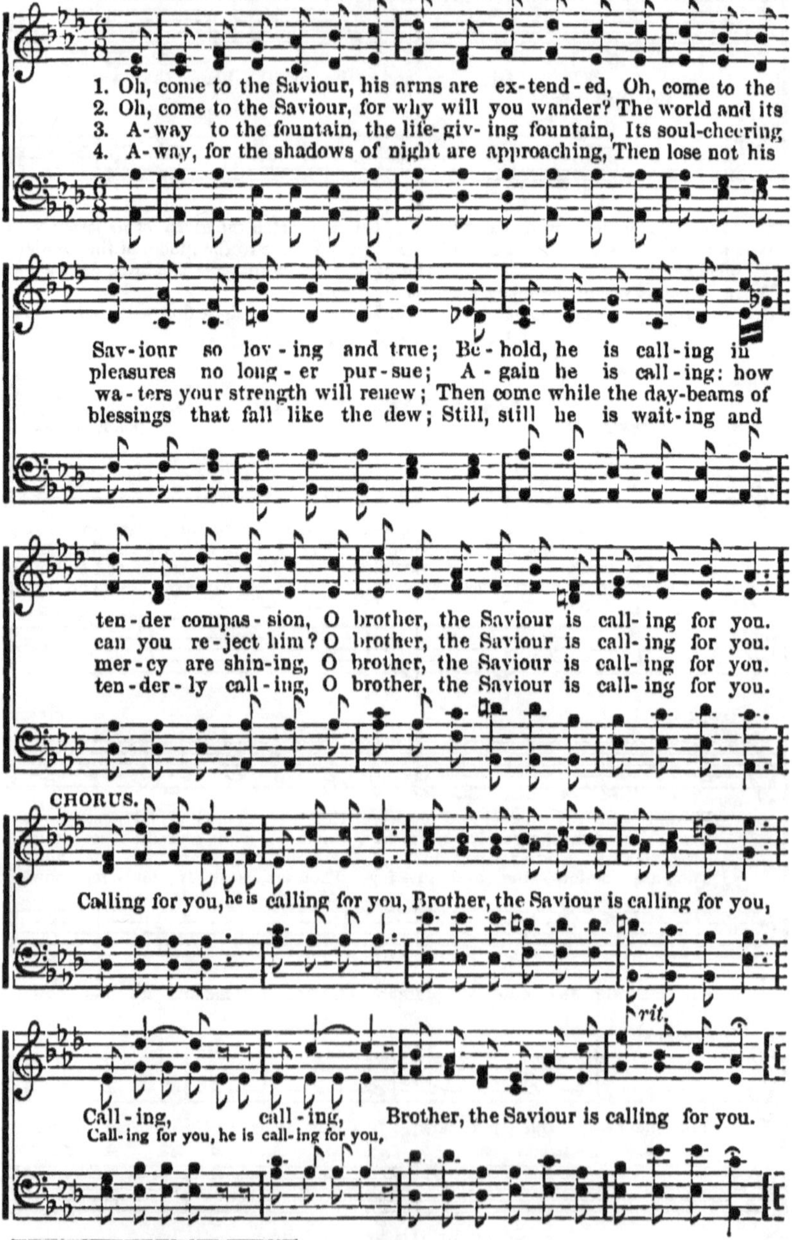

328. How can I live without Jesus.

"*Lo, I am with you alway, even unto the end of the world.*"—MARK xxviii. 20.
"*Without me ye can do nothing.*"—JN. xv. 5.

Mrs. EMMA PITT. WM. J. KIRKPATRICK.

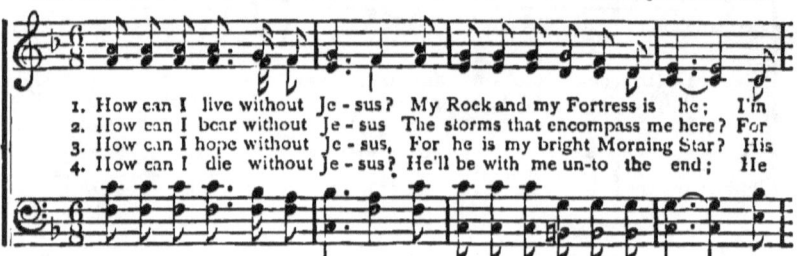

1. How can I live without Je-sus? My Rock and my Fortress is he; I'm
2. How can I bear without Je-sus The storms that encompass me here? For
3. How can I hope without Je-sus, For he is my bright Morning Star? His
4. How can I die without Je-sus? He'll be with me un-to the end; He

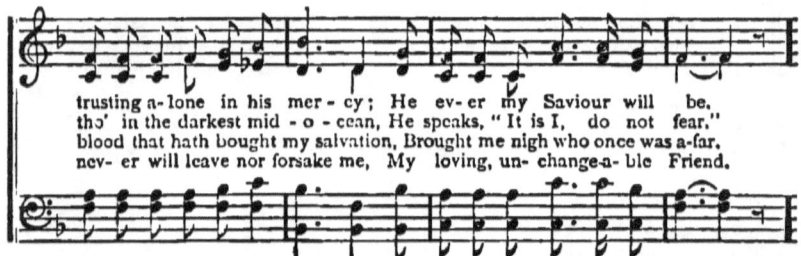

trusting a-lone in his mer-cy; He ev-er my Saviour will be.
tho' in the darkest mid-o-cean, He speaks, "It is I, do not fear."
blood that hath bought my salvation, Brought me nigh who once was a-far.
nev-er will leave nor forsake me, My loving, un-change-a-ble Friend.

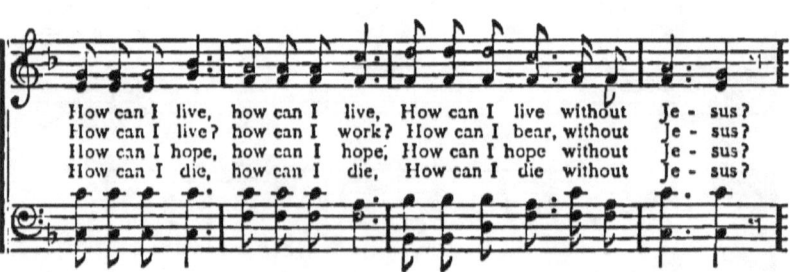

How can I live, how can I live, How can I live without Je-sus?
How can I live? how can I work? How can I bear, without Je-sus?
How can I hope, how can I hope, How can I hope without Je-sus?
How can I die, how can I die, How can I die without Je-sus?

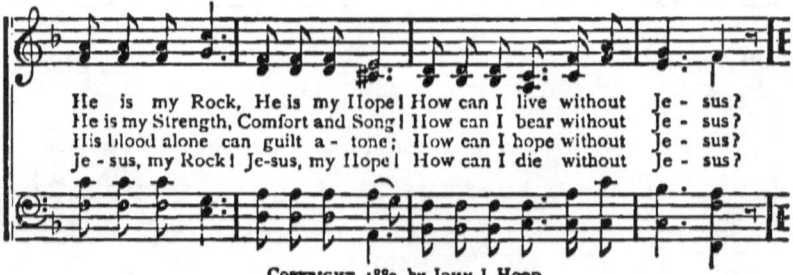

He is my Rock, He is my Hope! How can I live without Je-sus?
He is my Strength, Comfort and Song! How can I bear without Je-sus?
His blood alone can guilt a-tone; How can I hope without Je-sus?
Je-sus, my Rock! Je-sus, my Hope! How can I die without Je-sus?

COPYRIGHT, 1880, by JOHN J. HOOD.

329. Waiting for the Light.

Jno R. Sweney.

1. I am waiting, O my Father, For the coming of the light,—
   For the sunshine of thy presence, That shall lift the clouds of night.
2. I am waiting, blessed Saviour, Let thy presence light my way,
   Let thy loving hand e'er lead me, Let me never from thee stray.
3. I am waiting, Lord, why tarry? Enter quick the open door,
   Let me feel that thou art with me, And I ask for nothing more.
4. I am waiting, O my Father, Yet I see the coming light,
   Yet I feel thy tender presence, Nevermore shall it be night.

CHORUS.
I am waiting, I am waiting for thy footstep, As it comes, yes, as it comes toward my door;
O, my Father, enter quickly, Leave me never, nevermore.

---

330. That Beautiful Land.

Key Bb.

1 A BEAUTIFUL land by faith I see,
  A land of rest from sorrow free:
  The home of the ransomed, bright and fair,
  And beautiful angels, too, are there.

Cho.—Will you go? will you go?
  Go to that beautiful land with me?
  Will you go? will you go?
  Go to that beautiful land.

2 That land is called the City of Light;
  It never has known the shades of night:
  The glory of God, the light of day,
  Hath driven the darkness far away.

3 In vision I see its streets of gold,
  Its gates of pearl I, too, behold;
  The river of life, the crystal sea,
  The ambrosial fruit of life's fair tree.

4 The ransomed throng, arrayed in white,
  In rapture range the plains of light;
  In one harmonious choir they praise
  Their glorious Saviour's matchless grace.

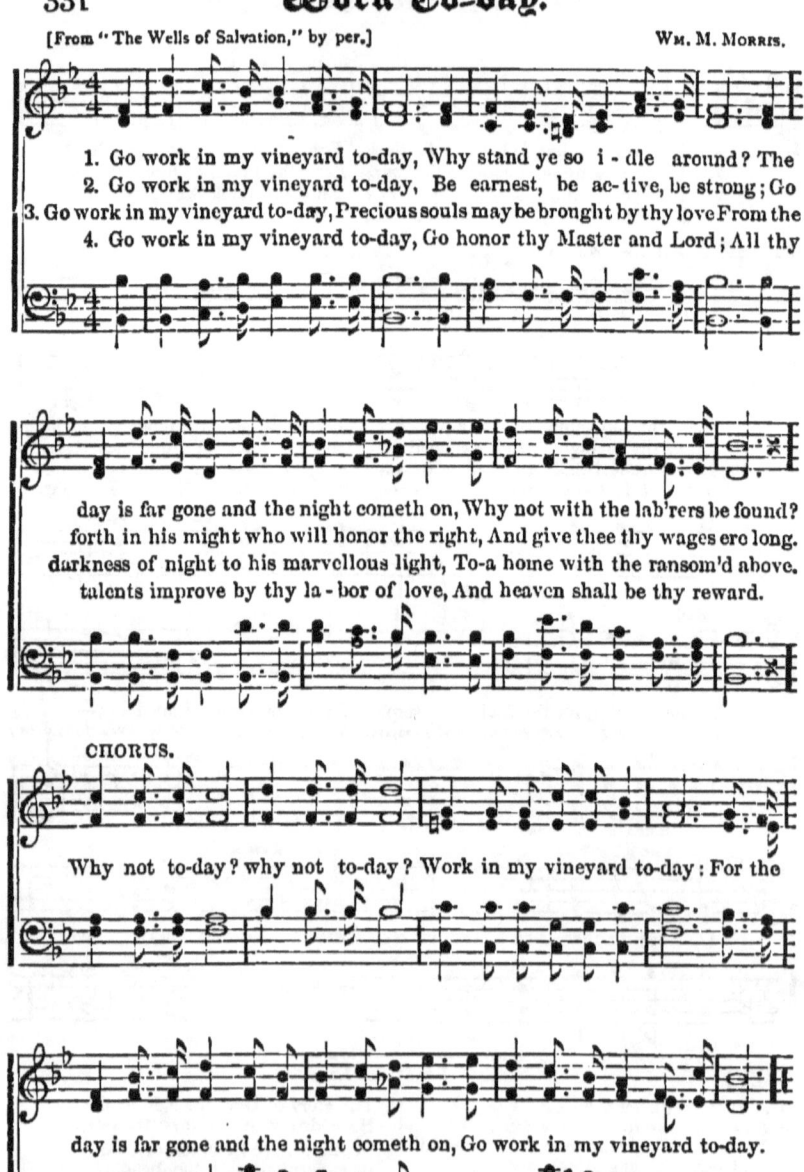

333. Resting on the Lord.

"Help us, O Lord our God; for we rest on thee, and in thy name go against this multitude."
2 Chron. xiv. 11.

Chas. H. Gabriel.   Wm. J. Kirkpatrick.

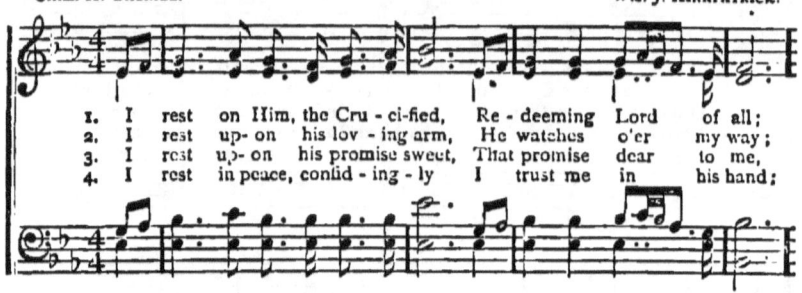

1. I rest on Him, the Cru-ci-fied, Re-deeming Lord of all;
2. I rest up-on his lov-ing arm, He watches o'er my way;
3. I rest up-on his promise sweet, That promise dear to me,
4. I rest in peace, confid-ing-ly I trust me in his hand;

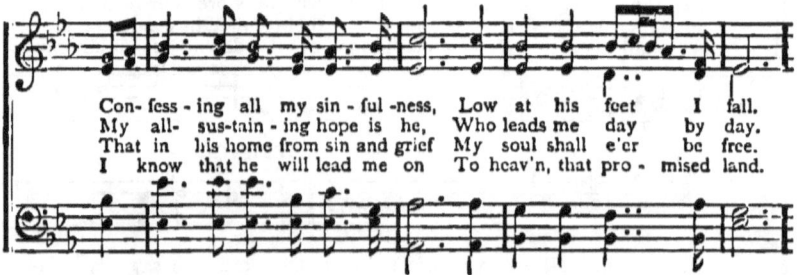

Con-fess-ing all my sin-ful-ness, Low at his feet I fall.
My all- sus-tain-ing hope is he, Who leads me day by day.
That in his home from sin and grief My soul shall e'er be free.
I know that he will lead me on To heav'n, that pro-mised land.

CHORUS.

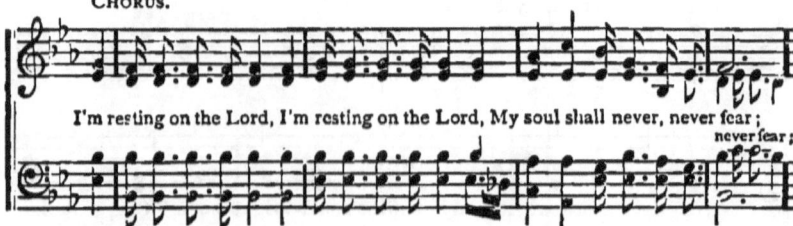

I'm resting on the Lord, I'm resting on the Lord, My soul shall never, never fear;

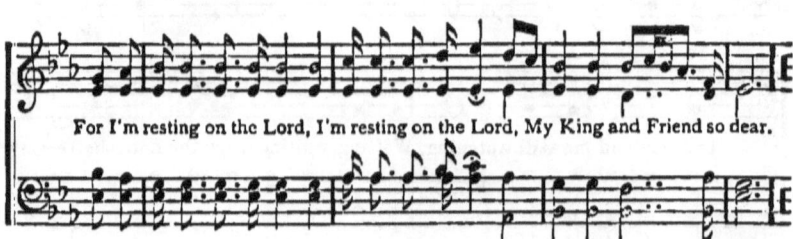

For I'm resting on the Lord, I'm resting on the Lord, My King and Friend so dear.

Copyright, 1880, by John J. Hood.

336 Shall We Meet?

H. L. Hastings.   Elisha S. Rice.

1. Shall we meet beyond the river, Where the surges cease to roll?
Where in all the bright forever, Sorrow ne'er shall press the soul?

2. Shall we meet in that blest harbor, When our stormy voyage is o'er?
Shall we meet and cast the anchor By the bright celestial shore?

D.S. Shall we meet beyond the river, Where the surges cease to roll?

Chorus.
Shall we meet, shall we meet, Shall we meet beyond the river?

3 Shall we meet in yonder city,
   Where the towers of crystal shine?
Where the walls are all of jasper,
   Built by workmanship divine?

4 Where the music of the ransomed
   Rolls its harmony around,
And creation swells the chorus
   With its sweet melodious sound?

5 Shall we meet there many a loved one,
   That was torn from our embrace?
Shall we listen to their voices,
   And behold them face to face?

6 Shall we meet with Christ our Saviour,
   When he comes to claim his own?
Shall we know his blessed favor,
   And sit down upon his throne?

337 The Land of the Blest.   Tune, "In the sweet by and by."

1 WE speak of the land of the blest,
   A country so bright and so fair,
And oft are its glories confest,
   But what must it be to be there.

Chorus.— In the sweet by and by,
   We shall meet on that beautiful shore,
In the sweet by and by,
   We shall meet on that beautiful shore.

2 We speak of its pathways of gold,
   Its walls decked with jewels so rare,
Its wonders and pleasures untold,
   But what must it be to be there.

3 We speak of its peace and its love,
   The robes which the glorified wear,
The songs of the blessed above,
   But what must it be to be there.

4 We speak of its freedom from sin,
   From sorrow, temptation, and care,
From trials without and within,
   But what must it be to be there.

5 Do thou, Lord, midst pleasure or woe,
   For heaven our spirits prepare,
Then shortly we also shall know,
   And feel what it is to be there.

By and by.—CONCLUDED.

peat, Cast our crowns at Jesus' feet, By and by, by and by.

344. Jesus is Mine.

[From "The Wells of Salvation," by per.]
Wm. J. Kirkpatrick.

1. Now I have found a Friend; Jesus is mine! His love shall never end; Jesus is mine! Tho' earthly joys decrease, Tho' human friendships cease, Now I have lasting peace; Jesus is mine!
2. When earth shall pass away Jesus is mine! In the great judgment day, Jesus is mine! Oh! what a glorious thing, Then to behold my King, On tuneful harp to sing, Jesus is mine!
3. Farewell, Mortality Jesus is mine! Welcome, Eternity; Jesus is mine! He my Redeemer is, Wisdom and Righteousness, Life, Light, and Holiness; Jesus is mine!
4. Father, thy name I bless; Jesus is mine! Thine was the sovereign grace; Jesus is mine! Spirit of Holiness, Sealing the Father's grace, Thou needst my soul embrace, Jesus is mine!

Copyright, 1881, by John J. Hood.

351. **Keep Looking unto Jesus.**

PRISCILLA J. OWENS. [From "The Wells of Salvation," by per.] WM. J. KIRKPATRICK.

1. Keep looking un-to Je-sus as we march a-long, Keep looking un-to
2. Keep looking un-to Je-sus with the night around, Keep looking un-to
3. Keep looking un-to Je-sus when the storms are out, Keep looking unto
4. Keep looking un-to Je-sus, Author of our faith, Keep looking un-to

Jesus all the day, When our hopes are steadfast and our hearts are strong,
Je-sus, Star and Sun. We shall yet behold him with full glo-ry crowned,
Je-sus, sore-ly tried; We shall win the bat-tle with a song and shout;
Je-sus as we move, We shall share his triumph ov-er sin and death,

CHORUS.

We can tread the nar-row way. Keep looking un-to Je-sus,
When the fi-nal vic-t'ry's won.
We shall find new strength sup-plied.
We shall reign with him a-bove.

looking un-to Je-sus, Looking un-to Je-sus ev-'ry day. Till our

cares grow lighter and our hopes grow brighter, And our sorrows flee away.

Copyright, 1881, by JOHN J. HOOD.

353. Rejoicing Evermore.

JOHN NEWTON. R. E. HUDSON.

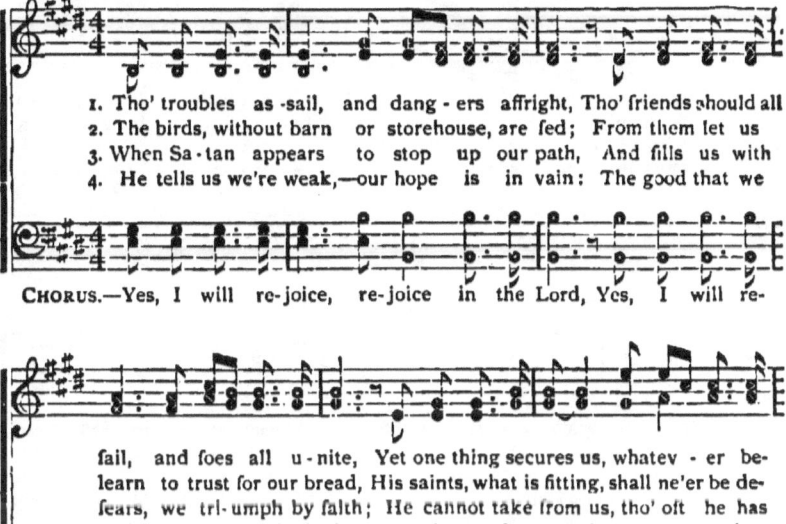

1. Tho' troubles as-sail, and dang-ers affright, Tho' friends should all fail, and foes all u-nite, Yet one thing secures us, whatev-er be-tide, The prom-ise as-sures us,—the Lord will pro-vide.
2. The birds, without barn or storehouse, are fed; From them let us learn to trust for our bread, His saints, what is fitting, shall ne'er be de-nied, So long as 'tis written,—the Lord will pro-vide.
3. When Sa-tan appears to stop up our path, And fills us with fears, we tri-umph by faith; He cannot take from us, tho' oft he has tried, The heart-cheer-ing promise,—the Lord will pro-vide.
4. He tells us we're weak,—our hope is in vain: The good that we seek we ne'er shall obtain: But when such suggestions our graces have tried, This ans-wers all questions,—the Lord will pro-vide.

CHORUS.—Yes, I will re-joice, re-joice in the Lord, Yes, I will re-joice, re-joice in the Lord, Yes, I will re-joice, re-joice in the Lord, Will joy in the God of my sal-va-tion.

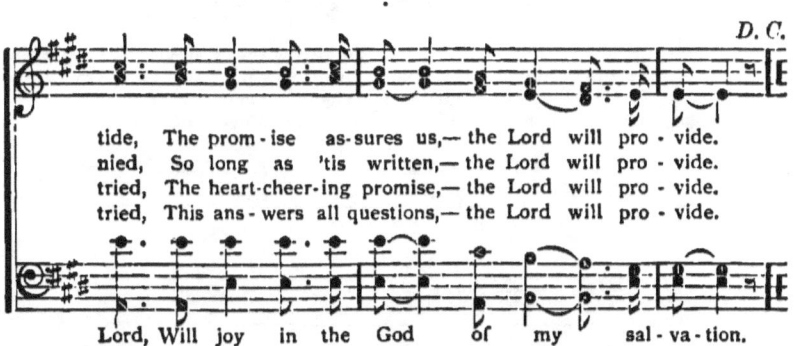

5 No strength of our own, nor goodness we claim;
Our trust is all thrown on Jesus' great name;
In this our strong tower for safety we hide;
The Lord is our power,—the Lord will provide.

6 When life sinks apace, and death is in view,
The word of his grace shall comfort us through:
Not fearing or doubting, with Christ on our side,
We hope to die shouting,—the Lord will provide.

From "Salvation Echoes," by per.

356. It is Good to be Here.

Rev. I. N. Wilson.   Jno. R. Sweney, by per.

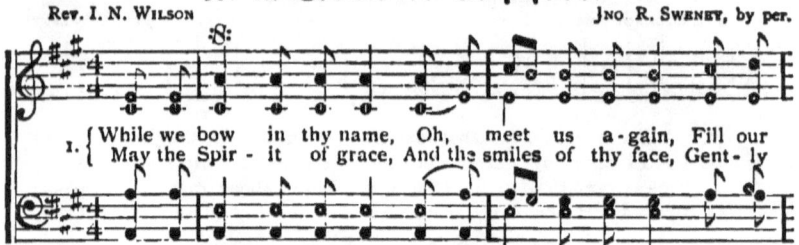

1. { While we bow in thy name, Oh, meet us a-gain, Fill our
    May the Spir-it of grace, And the smiles of thy face, Gent-ly
hearts with the light of thy love; }
fall on us now from a-bove.   } It is good to be here, it is
good for us, Lord, to be here.

D. S.—light streaming down makes the pathway all clear, It is good to be here, Thy perfect love now drives a-way all our fear, And

2 Our souls long for thee;
  Oh, may we now see
A sin-cleansing blood-wave appear;
  And feel, as it rolls
  In power o'er our souls,
It is good for us, Lord, to be here.

3 Thou art with us, we know;
  We feel the sweet flow [tide;
Of the sin-cleansing wave's gladd'ning
  We are washed from our sin,
  Made all holy within,
And in Jesus we sweetly abide.

Copyright, 1879, by Jno. R. Sweney.

357.   OH, HOW HAPPY ARE THEY.   Tune and Chorus above.

Oh, how happy are they
  Who the Saviour obey,
And have laid up their treasures above;
  Tongue can never express
  The sweet comfort and peace
Of a soul in its earliest love.

2 That sweet comfort was mine,
  When the favor divine
I received thro' the blood of the Lamb;
  When my heart first believed,
  What a joy I received—
What a heaven in Jesus' name!

3 'Twas a heaven below
  My Redeemer to know,
And the angels could do nothing more
  Than to fall at his feet,
  And the story repeat,
And the Lover of sinners adore.

4 Jesus, all the day long,
  Was my joy and my song;
Oh, that all his salvation might see:
  He hath loved me, I cried,
  He hath suffered and died,
To redeem even rebels like me.

4 The Father hears him pray,
  His dear anointed One;
He cannot turn away
  The presence of his Son:
His Spirit answers to the blood,
And tells me I am born of God.

5 My God is reconciled;
  His pard'ning voice I hear:
He owns me for his child;
  I can no longer fear:
With confidence I now draw,
And, "Father, Abba, Father," cry.

363. Is not this the Land of Beulah.

ANON. ARRANGED.

1. I am dwell-ing on the mountain, Where the gold-en sunlight gleams
2. I can see far down the mountain, Where I wandered wea-ry years,
3. I am drink-ing at the fountain, Where I ev-er would a-bide;

O'er a land whose wondrous beauty Far ex-ceeds my fondest dreams;
Oft-en hin-dered in my jour-ney By the ghosts of doubts and fears,
For I've tast-ed life's pure riv-er, And my soul is sat-is-fied;

Where the air is pure, e-the-real, Laden with the breath of flowers,
Brok-en vows and dis-appointments Thickly sprinkled all the way,
There's no thirst-ing for life's pleasures, Nor a-dorn-ing, rich and gay,

CHO.—Is not this the land of Beu-lah, Blessed, bles-sed land of light,

D. S. Chorus.

They are blooming by the fountain, 'Neath the am-a-ranthine bowers.
But the Spir-it led, un-er-ring, To the land I hold to-day.
For I've found a rich-er treasure, One that fad-eth not a-way.

Where the flow-ers bloom for-ev-er, And the sun is always bright.

4 Tell me not of heavy crosses,
  Nor the burdens hard to bear,
For I've found this great salvation
  Makes each burden light appear;
And I love to follow Jesus,
  Gladly counting all but dross,
Worldly honors all forsaking
  For the glory of the Cross.

5 Oh, the Cross has wondrous glory!
  Oft I've proved this to be true;
When I'm in the way so narrow
  I can see a pathway through;
And how sweetly Jesus whispers:
  Take the Cross, thou need'st not fear,
For I've tried this way before thee,
  And the glory lingers near.

What a Gath'ring, etc.—CONCLUDED

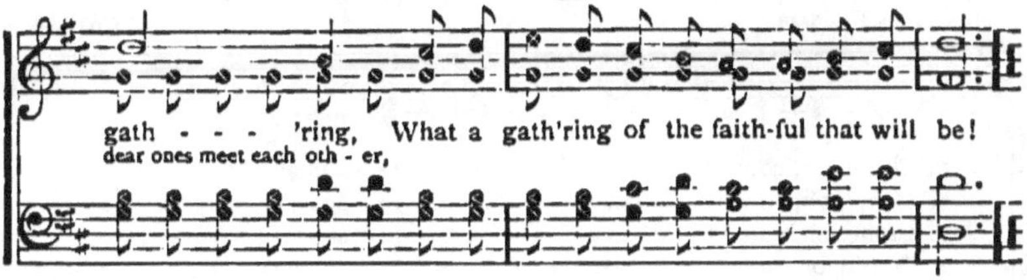
gath - - - 'ring, What a gath'ring of the faith-ful that will be!
dear ones meet each oth - er,

368 Oh! 'tis Glory in My Soul.

Flora L. Best. Jno. R. Sweney.

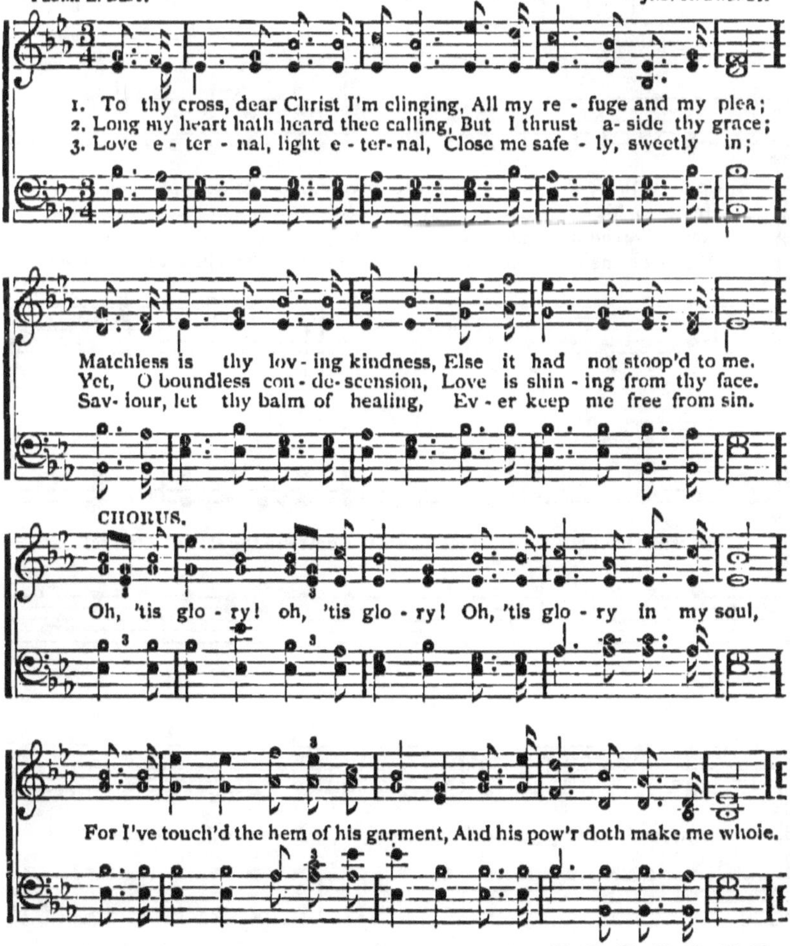
1. To thy cross, dear Christ I'm clinging, All my re - fuge and my plea;
2. Long my heart hath heard thee calling, But I thrust a- side thy grace;
3. Love e - ter - nal, light e - ter- nal, Close me safe - ly, sweetly in;
Matchless is thy lov - ing kindness, Else it had not stoop'd to me.
Yet, O boundless con - de- scension, Love is shin - ing from thy face.
Sav- iour, let thy balm of healing, Ev - er keep me free from sin.
CHORUS.
Oh, 'tis glo - ry! oh, 'tis glo - ry! Oh, 'tis glo - ry in my soul,
For I've touch'd the hem of his garment, And his pow'r doth make me whole.

By permission.

DO RE MI FA SO LA SI

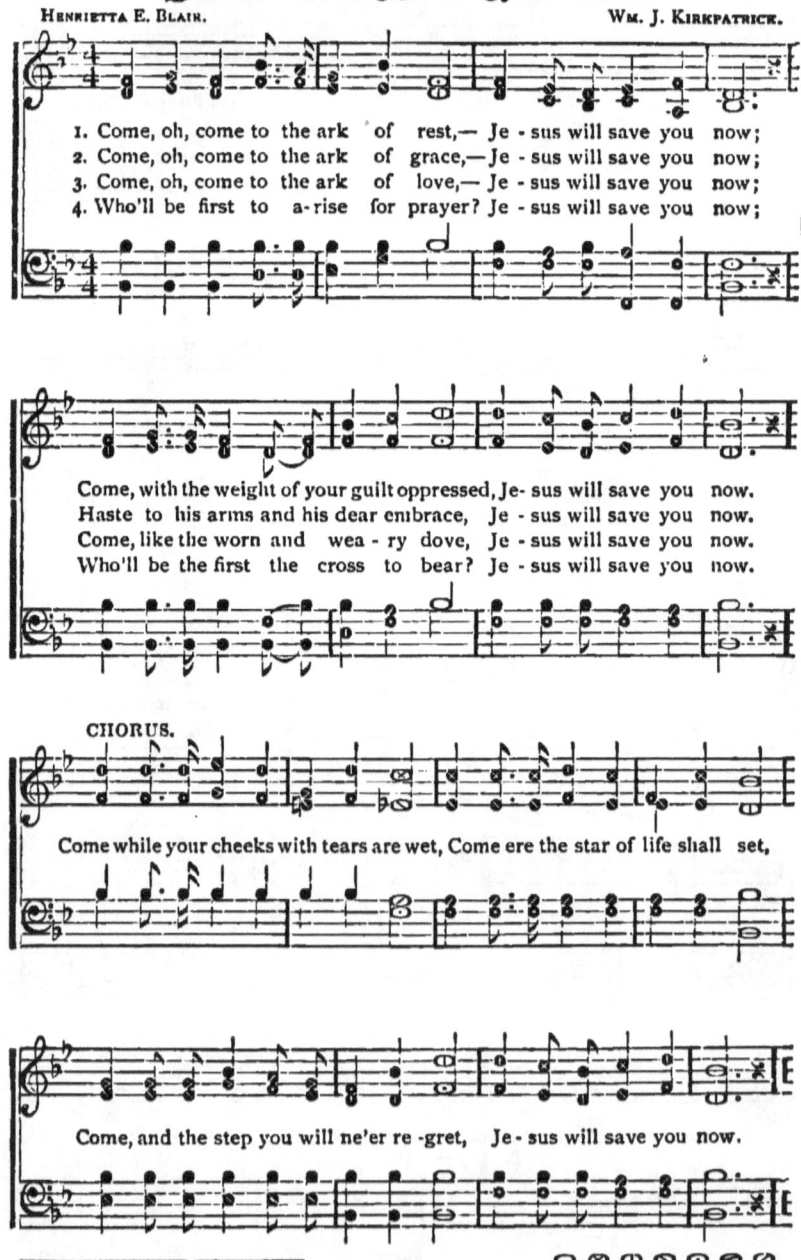

370. Glorious Fountain.

COWPER. T. C. O'KANE.

1. There is a fountain filled with blood, filled with blood, filled with blood, There is a fountain filled with blood, Drawn from Imman-uel's veins,
And sinners plung'd beneath that flood, beneath that flood, beneath that flood, And sinners plunged beneath that flood, Lose all their guilt-y stains.
2. The dy-ing thief rejoiced to see, rejoiced to see, rejoiced to see, The dy-ing thief rejoiced to see That fount-ain in his day,
And there may I, tho' vile as he, tho' vile as he, tho' vile as he, And there may I, tho' vile as he, Wash all my sins a-way.

CHORUS.
Oh, glo-ri-ous fount-ain! Here will I stay, And in thee ev-er Wash my sins a-way.

3 Thou dying Lamb, ‖: thy precious blood :‖
Shall never lose its power,
Till all the ransomed ‖:Church of God ‖
Are saved, to sin no more.

4 E'er since by faith ‖: I saw the stream ‖
Thy flowing wounds supply,
Redeeming love ‖: has been my theme,:‖
And shall be till I die.

371. Stand up! stand up for Jesus!

Tune, "Webb," Key Bb.

1 STAND up! stand up for Jesus!
Ye soldiers of the cross;
Lift high his royal banner,
It must not suffer loss;
From victory unto victory
His army he shall lead,
Till every foe is vanquished,
And Christ is Lord indeed.

2 Stand up! stand up for Jesus!
Stand in his strength alone;
The arm of flesh will fail you,—
Ye dare not trust your own;
Put on the gospel armor,
Each piece put on with prayer,
Where duty calls, or danger,
Be never wanting there.

3 Stand up! stand up for Jesus!
The strife will not be long;
This day the noise of battle,
The next the victor's song;
To him that overcometh
A crown of life shall be,
He with the King of glory
Shall reign eternally.

376. Keep me ever close to Thee.

FANNY J. CROSBY.   WM. J. KIRKPATRICK.

1. Source from whence the streams of mercy Like a riv-er flow to me,
2. There my life, my hope and com-fort, There a ref-uge for my soul
3. There, in ho-ly, sweet com-munion With thy Spir-it day by day,
4. Close to thee, O Saviour, keep me, Till I reach the shin-ing shore,—

With thy cords of love so ten-der Bind and keep me close to thee.
When the clouds hang dark-ly round me, And the dis-tant surg-es roll.
Faith to realms of light and glo-ry Bears my rap-tured soul a-way.
Till I join the raptured ar-my, Shouting joy for ev-er-more.

REFRAIN.

Keep me ev-er close to thee, Blessed Saviour, dear to me, With thy cords of love so tender Bind and keep me close to thee; Keep me ev-er close to thee, Blessed Sav-iour, dear to me, Bind and keep me close to thee.

Copyright, 1880, by JOHN J. HOOD.

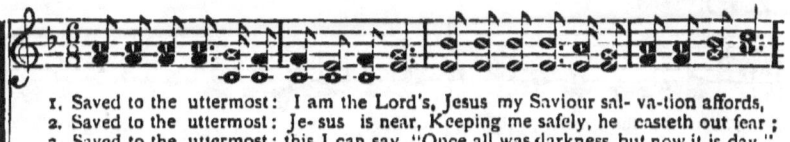

383. Triumph By and by.

Dr. C. R. Blackall. H. R. Palmer.

1. The prize is set be-fore us, To win, his words implore us, The eye of God is o'er us, From on high, *from on high;* His loving tones are calling, While sin is dark, appalling; 'Tis Jesus gently calling, He is nigh, *he is nigh.*

2. We'll fol-low where he lead-eth, We'll past-ure where he feed-eth, We'll yield to him who pleadeth From on high, *from on high;* Then naught from him shall sever, Our hope shall brighten ever, And faith shall fail us nev-er, He is nigh, *he is nigh.*

3. Our home is bright a-bove us, No tri-als dark to move us, But Jesus, dear, to love us, There on high, *there on high;* We'll give him best endeavor, And praise his name forever; His precious ones can never, Nev-er die, *never die.*

CHORUS.

By and by we shall meet him, By and by we shall greet him, And with Jesus reign in glory, By and by, *by and by;* Jesus reign in glory, By and by.

By permission. 345

384. When I'm Happy.

Arr. by W. J. K.

1. When I'm hap-py, hear me sing, When I'm happy, hear me sing, When I'm happy, hear me sing, Give me Jesus, Give me Jesus, Give me Jesus; You may have all the world: Give me Jesus.
2. When in sor-row, hear me pray, When in sorrow, hear me pray, When in sorrow, hear me pray, Give me Jesus,
3. When I'm dy-ing, hear me cry, When I'm dying, hear me cry, When I'm dying, hear me cry, Give me Jesus,
4. When I'm ris-ing, hear me shout, When I'm rising, hear me shout, When I'm rising, hear me shout Give me Jesus,
5. When in heav-en, we will sing, When in heav-en, we will sing, When in heaven, we will sing, Blessed Jesus, Bles-sed Jesus, Bles-sed Jesus, By thy grace we are saved, Bles-sed Jesus.

Copyright, 1886, by JOHN J. HOOD.

385. O when shall I see Jesus.

1 O WHEN shall I see Jesus,
    And dwell with him above—
  To drink the flowing fountain
    Of everlasting love?
  When shall I be delivered
    From this vain world of sin,
  And with my blessed Jesus
    Drink endless pleasures in?

Cho.—Then palms of victory, crowns of
    glory,
  Palms of victory I shall wear. :||

2 But now I am a soldier,
    My Captain's gone before;
  He's given me my orders,
    And tells me not to fear;
  And if I hold out faithful
    A crown of life he'll give,
  And all his valiant soldiers
    Eternal life shall have.

3 O, do not be discouraged,
    For Jesus is your Friend,
  And if you lack for knowledge,
    He'll not refuse to lend;
  Neither will he upbraid you,
    Though often you request;
  He'll give you grace to conquer,
    And take you home to rest.

386. Entire Consecration.

Frances Ridley Havergal.   Wm. J. Kirkpatrick.

1. Take my life, and let it be Con-se-crated, Lord, to thee;
2. Take my feet, and let them be Swift and beau-ti-ful for thee;
3. Take my lips, and let them be Filled with messag-es for thee;
4. Take my moments, and my days, Let them flow in endless praise;

Take my hands, and let them move At the impulse of thy love.
Take my voice, and let me sing Al-ways, on-ly, for my King.
Take my sil-ver and my gold,— Not a mite would I with-hold.
Take my in-te-lect, and use Ev'-ry pow'r as thou shalt choose.

Chorus.
{ Wash me in the Saviour's precious blood, *the precious blood,* }
{ Cleanse me in its pu-ri-fy-ing flood, *the healing flood,* }
Lord, I give to thee my life and all, to be Thine, hence-forth e-ter-nal-ly.

5 Take my will, and make it thine;
   It shall be no longer mine;
   Take my heart,—it is thine own,—
   It shall be thy royal throne.

6 Take my love,—my Lord, I pour
   At thy feet its treasure-store!
   Take myself, and I will be
   Ever, only, all for thee!

387 Whosoever.

James Nicholson. Jno. R. Sweney.

1. I praise the Lord that one like me For mer-cy may to Je-sus flee,
2. I was to sin a wretched slave, But Je-sus died my soul to save;
3. I look by faith and see this word, Stamp'd with the blood of Christ my Lord,
4. I now believe he saves my soul, His precious blood hath made me whole;

He says that who-so-ev-er will May seek and find sal-va-tion still.

CHORUS.

My Saviour's promise faileth never; He counts me in the Who-so-ev-er.

From "Gems of Praise," by per.

388 We Shall Know. Key Eb.

1 WHEN the mists have rolled in splendor
  From the beauty of the hills,
And the sunshine, warm and tender,
  Falls in kisses on the rills,
We may read love's shining letter
  In the rainbow of the spray,—
We shall know each other better
  When the mists have cleared away.

Cho.—We shall know as we are known,
  Never more to walk alone,
||: In the dawning of the morning,
  When the mists have cleared away. :||

2 If we err, in human blindness,
  And forget that we are dust;

If we miss the law of kindness
  When we struggle to be just,
Snowy wings of peace shall cover
  All the plain that hides away,—
When the weary watch is over,
  And the mists have cleared away.

3 When the mists have risen above us,
  As our Father knows his own,
Face to face with those that love us,
  We shall know as we are known;
Love, beyond the orient meadows
  Floats the golden fringe of day,
Heart to heart, we bide the shadows,
  Till the mists have cleared away.

INDEX

First Lines in roman; Titles in capitals.

	HYMN.		HYMN.		HYMN.
A beautiful land by faith	330	Blest be the tie that	161	FACE THE OTHER WAY	101
A better day is coming,	218	BREAD AND TO SPARE,	81	Faith builds her founda-	220
Ah! 'tis the old, old	150	Brother for Christ's king-	169	Faithful remain to thy	273
Alas! alas! a wayward	237	BRINGING IN THE	146	FALL INTO LINE,	65
Alas! and did my Sav-	257	BY AND BY,	343	Fall into line, brother	65
A little boy lay down to	287	BY THE GRACE OF GOD	59	FAR AS THE EAST	73
A little talk with Jesus,	250			Far away my steps have	92
A little while together	95	CALL AND I WILL	22	Far out on the desolate	192
A little while to sow and	108	Called to the feast by	364	FILL ME NOW,	325
A LITTLE WORD,	84	CALLING FOR YOU,	326	FLOW IN,	197
ALL ATONING BLOOD,	215	CALLING YOU AND ME,	226	FOLLOW JESUS,	231
All hail the power of	160	CALVARY,	41	Follow thou me, says a	80
ALL THE WAY LONG IT	129	Can you do without the	283	FOR ME, FOR ME,	135
Along the river of time.	120	Care for the desolate	25	FORWARD MARCH,	126
ALWAYS ABOUNDING	87	CAST THY BURDEN	149	FREE FROM SIN	32
Am I a soldier of the	271	Children of the heaven-	315	From Calvary's mount-	366
Amid these cares and	22	CHRIST AROSE,	98	From the gloom of un-	32
Amid the trials which	56	CHRIST FOR ME,	7	FROM THIS HOUR	30
ANY ONE HERE?,	345	Christ Jesus is my an-	243		
ARE YOU READY?	138	CHRIST SHALL REIGN	103	GENTLE SHEPHERD,	92
Are you ready for his	90	CLINGING TO THE	244	GIVE ME JESUS,	352
Are you ready for the	361	COME AND SEE,	93	GLORIOUS FOUNTAIN,	370
ARE YOU WASHED IN	377	Come, oh, come to the	369	GLORY TO HIS NAME,	292
Are you weary, are you	350	Come to Jesus,	142	GLORY TO JESUS FOR-	260
Are you willing to wan-	224	Come to the fount of	202	Go and preach the	112
Arise my soul, arise;	359	Come to the Rock, the	284	God be with you till we	293
A SHOUT IN THE CAMP,	235	COME TO THY FATHER	334	God has given me a song	213
A SINNER LIKE ME,	124	Come, ye sinners, poor	47, 335	God is giving, largely	86
A SMILE FROM JESUS,	338	Come, ye that love the	301	God loved the world	42
A SONG OF TRUST.	213	COMING HOME TO-DAY,	346	GOD SO LOVED THE	42
ASSURANCE,	359	COMING TO-DAY,	382	Go ye into all the world,	112
At home or abroad in	275	CONQUER BY AND BY,	205	Go work in my vineyard	331
AT HOME WITH JESUS,	217			Grace, 'tis a charming	298
A trembling soul I come	15	DEAR SAV'R, CLEANSE.	15	Grander than the billowy	248
AT THE CROSS I'LL A-	188	Depth of mercy; can	170		
At the feast of Belshaz-	71	Did Christ o'er sinners,	204	Hail, all hail, the Prince	2
At the gate that leads..	223	Do you know what	254	Hail, hail, hail, beautiful	104
At the sounding of the	367	Do you wonder that I	61	Hail to the brightness of	230
Awake, my soul, thy sa-	209	Down at the cross	292	HALLELUJAH, HE SAVE	318
AWAY TO JESUS,	108	DRAW ME TO THEE	134	Happy pilgrim, as you	231
		DRINKING AT THE	34	HAPPY TIDINGS,	364
BEAR A HAND,	286	DROPPING PENNIES,	38	Hark, hark, my soul,	114
Be earnest, my brothers,	87			Has the day been dark	291
BEFORE THE CROSS	166	EACH HEART THY	44	HAVE MERCY,	50
Before thee, O Father,	3	EDEN SHORE,	199	Have you been to Jesus	377
Behold a stranger at the	374	ENTIRE CONSECRATION	386	HEALING FOR THEE	115
BEHOLD THE BRIDE-	361	Eternity!—where?	66	Hear the earnest invita-	216
BEHOLD, THE FIELDS	253	Evening shades around	276	Hear the gentle voice	37
BELIEVING AND RE-	225	EVEN ME,	156	Hear the pennies drop-	38
BEULAH LAND,	182	EVER SINGING,	13	HEAR US, O FATHER,	3
Blessed Saviour, my	5	EVERY DAY,	99	He leadeth me! O bless-	173
Blest are the pure in	300	Every day my soul is hap-	262	HELP JUST A LITTLE,	169

349

HE WEPT FOR ME,	204	IS NOT THIS THE LAND	363	LEAN ON HIM,	232
HE WILL GATHER THE	317	I sought for the blessing	240	LET HIM IN,	148
HIS CHILD I WANT TO	85	I stand beside the crim-	268	LET THE MASTER IN,	342
Ho! every one that	236	Is that a cry from a storm	286	Lift the voice in holy	105
HOPE'S BRIGHT STAR,	104	IS THERE ANY ONE	79	LIFT UP YOUR VOICE	9
Hover o'er me, Holy	325	Is there any sad heart	345	Light after darkness	151
How blest was the life	242	IT IS GOOD TO BE HERE	356	Light in our darkness	125
How can I live without	328	IT IS WELL WITH MY	117	Like Jacob in his Bethel	40
How happy every child	309	I TRUST IN THEE,	45	Linger not, linger not,	36
How gentle God's com-	162	I've been to the field	11	LITTLE FRIENDS OF JE	254
How lovely is Jesus, the	320	I've reached the land	182	Little voices, happy	119
How sweet the name	155	I want to be a worker,	20	Living for Jesus, living	219
HUNG'RING AND	113	I was once far away	124	LOOK ALOFT,	91
		I will bless the Lord at	62	Looking unto Jesus,	4
I AM COMING,	74	I will look to the hills,	186	Look not on the clouds	16
I am dwelling on the	363	I will sing of my Re-	118	LOOK TO JESUS,	373
I AM GLAD,	107	I will sing when morning	24	LOOK TO JESUS NOW,	189
I am happy in the Lord,	241	I will tell the world a-	107	Look unto me and be	189
I am ransomed by the	289	I WILL TRUST IN THEE	5	Look up! behold the	253
I am saved! the Lord	355			Look upon the fields all	190
I am saved, yes, I'm	225	JESUS AT THE DOOR,	37	Lord, I am thine, entire-	314
I AM THINE,	341	JESUS DID IT,	265	Lord, I care not for	132
I am trusting in the	259	JESUS HAS DIED FOR	257	Lord, I come repenting,	51
I am walking with the	212	Jesus high in glory,	106	Lord, I hear of showers	156
I am waiting. O my F	329	Jesus, I come to thee,	100, 222	Lord, my wayward heart	362
I believe in God the	294	Jesus I love, for his	183	Lord, weak and im-	134
I'd rather get down at	233	JESUS IS GOOD TO ME,	183	LOST BUT FOUND,	321
I have come just now	193	JESUS IS MINE,	344	Lo! the day is breaking	89
I HAVE ENTERED BEU-	76	Jesus is pleading with	116	Low in the grave he lay,	98
I have found a friend	157	Jesus is waiting to save,	319		
I have found a friend in	280	JESUS KNOCKING,	263	MAKE ROOM FOR ME,	287
I have found a place for	58	JESUS LIVES FOREVER,	60	MAKING MELODY,	24
I have surrendered to	214	Jesus, lover of my soul,	178	MARCHING ON,	211
I heard the voice of Je-	310	JESUS LOVES ME SO,	347	March steadily onward	247
I hear thy welcome	171	Jesus, my faith 1 now	45	MEETING AND GATH-	46
I hope to meet you all	180	JESUS MY LORD,	233	MEET ME AT THE	122
I KNOW THAT HE LIV-	242	Jesus, my only hope,	27	MIGHTY JESUS SAVES,	67
I know that my Redeem-	53	JESUS OUR REDEEMER,	187	MORE AND MORE	86
I'LL LIVE FOR HIM,	288	JESUS SAVES,	354	MORE FAITH IN JE-	181
I'll never let go the an-	39	Jesus shed his precious	135	Mourn for the thousands	307
I love my Saviour dear,	347	Jesus the mighty conq'.	281	My brother, we are trav-	194
I love thy kingdom, Lord	297	Jesus the Saviour is pass	115	My country! 'tis of thee,	174
I love to tell the story	177	Jesus the Saviour is wait	358	My faith looks up to	166
I'M HOLDING ON,	380	Jesus wept! those tears,	249	My Father is rich in	144
I'm on my way to glory	201	JESUS WILL HELP YOU,	339	My God, thy mercies	341
I'M REDEEMED,	379	JESUS WILL SAVE YOU.	369	My heart is fixed,	7
In a world so full of	375	Journeying homeward,	234	MY HOPE AND MY GLO-	212
INFANT PRAISES,	106	JOY BELLS,	69	My life, my love I give	288
In perfect peace I now	8	JOY IN THE HEART,	184	My Lord and my	113
In the battlefield of life,	290	Joy! joy! joy! wonder-	103	MY REDEEMER,	118
IN THE BOOK OF LIFE,	64	Joy to the world,	306	My soul shall rejoice	94
In the darkest hour,	68	Just as I am, without	372	My way is dreary and	97
In the darkness, as I	272	Justified by faith in thee	187		
IN THE KING'S HIGH-.	221			NATURE'S LULLABY,	276
IN THE MORNING,	163	KEEP ME EVER CLOSE,	376	NATURE'S PRAISE,	77
In the murmur of the	77	Keep looking unto Je-.	351	Nearer, my God, to thee,	28
In the secret of his pres-	14	KEEP STEP EVER,	255	NEVER ALONE,	192
In thy book where	64	Keep thy faith steady,	63	NEVER DELAY,	36
Into the great beyond,	96			NO NIGHT THERE,	200
In vain in high and holy	185	Lamb of God, whose	48	Not here! not here!	121
I praise the Lord that	387	Leading souls to Jesus,	33	Now, boys, attend,	101
I rest on him, the cru-.	333	Lead me to Jesus, my	31	Now I have found a	344
IS MY NAME WRITTEN	132	LEANING ON JESUS	140		

INDEX.

Title	Page	Title	Page	Title	Page
O could I speak the	296	Peter on the troubled	67	Take my life and let it	386
O for a closer walk	72	PLEADING WITH THEE,	23	Take the world but give	352
O for a thousand tongues	305	PRAISE FOR A FULL	269	TELL IT TO JESUS,	350
O good old way, how	129	PRAISE THE LORD,	105	THE ANCHOR HOLDS,	243
O happy day, that fixed	167	PRAISE THE LORD JE-	2	THE ANGELS ARE	40
O happy day! what a	52	Praise the Lord with	252	THE APOSTLES CREED	294
Oh, bliss of the purified,	153	Pray for the fallen; oh,	57	THE BEAUTIFUL HILLS,	186
Oh, come, Holy Spirit,	196	Precious, precious blood	10	THE BOSOM OF MY	58
Oh, come to the S. be-	327	PRESS ONWARD,	208	THE CHILD OF A KING,	144
Oh, come to the S. his	326	Pretty, golden sunbeams	69	The children to Jesus	85
Oh, dying souls, look up,	373			THE COUNTERSIGN,	272
Oh, how happy are they,	357	Redeemed, how love to	245	THE CRIMSON STREAM,	268
Oh, I often sit and pon-	203	REDEEMED, PRAISE	52	The cross and the	55
Oh, my cup is overflow-	76	REFUGE,	68	THE CROSS FOREVER,	109
Oh, name of names the	228	REJOICING EVERMORE	353	THE FOUNTAIN FULL	236
Oh, sometimes the	239	REMEMBER CALVARY,	48	THE FOUNTAIN OF LIFE	193
Oh, speak to me, my Sav-	349	Repeat the story o'er	141	THE FOUNT OF MERCY	202
Oh, take the lamp of	246	REST,	251	THE FUTURE,	203
Oh, the joy that fills my	321	REST BY AND BY,	11	The golden spires are	19
Oh, think of the home	172	RESTING ON THE LORD	333	THE GREAT BEYOND,	96
OH, 'TIS GLORY IN	368	REVIVE THY WORK,	154	THE HANDWRITING	71
Oh, to be nearer,	322	Rock of ages, cleft for	165	THE HALF WAS NEVER	141
Oh, to be over yonder,	123	Room for my Saviour	110	The home-land! oh,	17
Oh, we'll meet and know	264	Rouse, ye saints, the	195	The K'ng as he stood	266
Oh, where are the reap-	278			THE LAMP OF FAITH,	245
Oh, why are you slight-	227	Sad and weary, lone	74	THE LILY OF THE VAL-	280
Oh, wondrous love that	256	SALVATION,	248	THE LORD'S PRAYER,	274
O Jesus Lord thy dy-	316	Salvation, O the joyful	304	THE LORD OF LIFE,	82
O Jesus, Saviour, I long	188	Saved to the uttermost	381	THE MIGHTY CONQUER	281
O life eternal, life divine	197	SAVE ME NOW,	362	THE NEW NAME,	133
O love divine, how sweet	295	Saviour, break this	26	THE NEW OVER THERE	340
O, my heart is full of	244	Saviour, like a shep-	176	THE NEW SONG,	324
O my Saviour, thou hast	215	See the faithful now re-	12	THE NUMBERLESS	102
O, my song is ever new	260	SHALL I BE SAVED TO-	116	THE OLD SHIP,	323
On Calvary's brow my	41	Shall we meet beyond	336	THE OPEN ARMS,	227
Once I heard a sound	342	SHINING FOR THEE,	75	THE PRINCE OF PEACE,	270
Once my eyes saw noth-	265	Should the summons,	138	The prize is set before.	383
One more day its twi-	175	SHOW ME THE ROCK,	26	There are songs of joy	324
On let us go where the	83	Simply trusting every	282	There is a fountain filled	370
Only a beam of sun-	229	Sing glory to God in the	318	There is joy in the heart	184
Only a look, my Sav-	378	SINGING GLORY,	201	There is a land of pure	179
ONLY HIS LOVE,	322	SING OF HIS MIGHTY	153	There is no night there,	200
ONLY REMEMBERED,	35	Sing with me of a Sav-.	1	There is pardon sweet	93
On my way to Zion,	13	Sing, ye people, loud	60	THE ROCK THAT IS	239
On the sweet Eden shore,	199	Sinner, to the Saviour	126	There's a light at the	75
On to the work! for the	277	SOLDIERS OF THE	271	There's a shout in the	235
ONWARD MARCH,	290	SONGS IN THE CALM,	88	There's a stranger at the	148
Onward now! the trum-	198	Sound, sound the jubilee	18	There's a thought that	111
OPEN THE DOOR,	358	Source from whence the	376	There's a voice in my	348
Open the door that so	263	Sowing in the morning,	146	There will be no sin nor	343
O prodigal, dont stay a-		Stand at your post,	136	The Saviour is calling	339
O RECEIVE HIM,	119	Stand up, and bless the	299	The Spirit and the	43
O Saviour, precious	9	Stand up! stand up for	371	THE STORY OF CLEANS	261
O sing of Jesus, Lamb	379	STAY NOT,	319	THE STRANGER AT	374
O that my load of sin	313	STEP OUT UPON THE	291	THE STRONG ONE,	54
O, turn not back in the	258	STRIVE TO ENTER IN	223	THE SUMMER LAND	269
Our Father who art in	274	Sun of my soul, thou	152	THE UNIVERSAL CALL,	43
Our heavenly habitation	217	SUNSHINE,	16	THE WAITING GUEST,	191
OUR REAPING SONG,	89	SURRENDERED,	214	The way is long and	50
Out on the desert, look-	382	Sweet hour of prayer,	168	THE WAY OF SALVA-	240
OUTSIDE THE FOLD,	97			The whole wide world	29
OVERCOMERS,	128	TAKE HOLD, HOLD ON,	258	THEY ARE COMING,	12
O when shall I see Je-	385	TAKE ME AS I AM,	372	They have reached the	340

THIS GOD IS OUR GOD	220	Up for Jesus; up and	78	When Jesus comes to re-	332
Thou chief among ten-.	44	Until his kingdom come,	206	When Jesus shall gather	317
Though kindred ties a-	338	UNTIL YE FIND, .	237	When our vessel is rock-	91
Though there may be .	99			When peace, like a river	117
Though troubles assail	353	VICTORY, .	127	When shall I look on .	207
THOUGHTS OF THE FU-	111	Victory through Jesus!	267	WHEN SHALL I SEE .	207
Though weak my faith .	380			When the clouds were .	49
THOU THINKEST, LORD	56	WAITING FOR THE .	329	WHEN THE KING .	364
THOU WILT DEFEND .	125	WAITING FOR YOU AND	19	When the mists have .	388
Through the gates of .	59	Walking with Jesus, my	365	When we enter the por-	102
Thus far the Lord hath .	312	Wand'rer from thy Fa-	334	While struggling thro' .	181
Tidings, happy tidings,	360	We are drinking at the	34	WHILE THE YEARS .	375
'Tis a story oft repeated	261	We are going, we are .	279	While we bow in thy .	356
'TIS SOME MOTHER'S .	275	We are looking away .	208	Who is this from Edom	54
'Tis the gospel message,	346	We are marching home	6	Who is this that wait- .	191
'Tis the Lord who lead-	88	We are on the deep, we	323	WHOSOEVER, .	387
'Tis the Shepherd's .	226	We are pilgrims looking	163	WHOSOEVER BELIEV-.	365
To Father, Son, and Ho-	304	We are praying, blessed	30	Whosoever will come .	21
To God, the Father, Son,	300	We are traveling on thro'	221	Who, who is he? .	128
To the house of his Fa-	81	Weary and thirsty, oh. .	23	Why art thou waiting?	285
To the summer-land of .	269	Weary pilgrim on life's	149	Why do you wait, dear	139
To thy cross, dear Christ	368	Weary with walking a- .	140	Why is thy harp on the	73
Touch my spirit with .	251	We have heard a joyful	354	WILL JESUS FIND US .	332
To us a child of hope is	303	We have taken up the .	205	WILL YOU COME? .	216
Trav'ling onward from .	46	WE'LL KNOW EACH .	264	WILL YOU GO? .	194
TRIUMPH BY AND BY,	383	We march to the field .	109	Will you meet me at the	122
Troubled heart, thy fear	232	We praise thee, O God .	154	With our colors waving	211
TRUE AND FAITHFUL,	262	We shall have a new .	133	WITNESSING SPIRIT, .	196
TRUSTING IN HIS WORD	259	We speak of the land of	337	WONDERFUL LOVE OF	185
Trusting in Jesus, my .	210	What a friend we have	164	WONDERFUL WORDS .	21
TRUSTING IN THE .	8	WHAT A GATHERING, .	367	WON'T YOU LOVE MY .	157
TRUSTING JESUS, THAT	282	What are these arrayed	127	Work, for the night is .	311
Trustingly, trustingly .	238	WHAT ARE YOU WILL-	224	WORK TO-DAY, .	331
'Twas a night of long a-	270	What glorious truth is .	82	Would you gain the best	255
'Twas spoken by the .	84	What glory gilds the .	302		
		What if your own were	70	YES, I WILL GO, .	348
Up and away, like the .	35	What ruin hath intem-	308	YES, THERE IS PARDON,	327
UP AND ONWARD, .	78	When I'm happy, hear	384	YOUR OWN, .	70